The LETTER

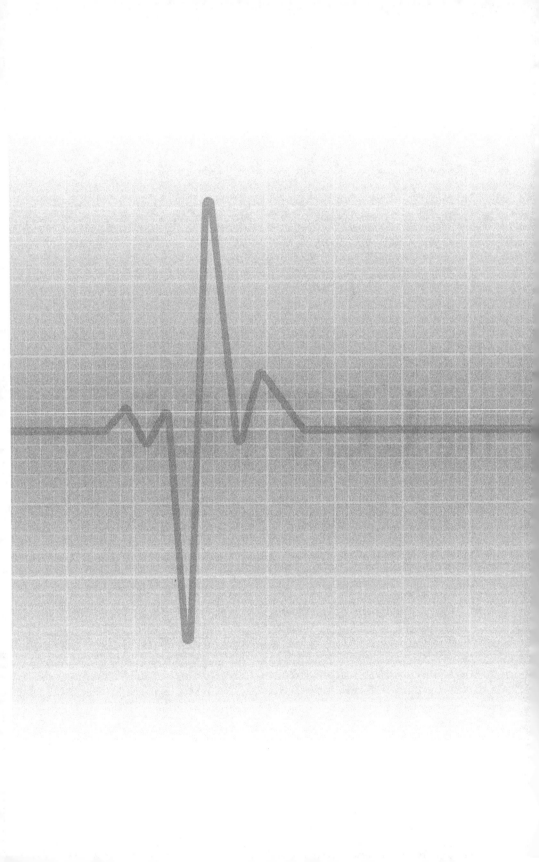

The LETTER

A Medical Doctor's Remarkable
Journey of Enduring Hope...

Diane VanHorne MD

XULON PRESS ELITE

Xulon Press Elite
2301 Lucien Way #415
Maitland, FL 32751
407.339.4217
www.xulonpress.com

© 2020 by Diane VanHorne MD

All rights reserved solely by the author. The author guarantees all contents are original and do not infringe upon the legal rights of any other person or work. No part of this book may be reproduced in any form without the permission of the author. The views expressed in this book are not necessarily those of the publisher.

Unless otherwise indicated, Scripture quotations taken from the King James Version (KJV) – *public domain.*

Scripture quotations taken from the Contemporary English Version (CEV). Copyright © 1995 American Bible Society. Used by permission. All rights reserved.

Paperback ISBN-13: 978-1-6312-9831-8

Hard Cover ISBN-13: 978-1-6312-9832-5
Ebook ISBN-13: 978-1-6312-9833-2

Dedication

To my sons and daughter, Max, Matthew and Sarah.

To my beloved grandma-ma, Dorosita, the single most consequential person in helping me become the woman I am today.

To the memory of Alan Jones, a treasure at the beginning of my journey.

I owe special thanks to:

Santiago, my husband, for his timeless support.

My sister Nancy, a true cheerleader who always believed in me.

My church family whose prayers got me through.

Ms. Claudette, Loida, Karen, Delrose, Otti, Michele, for their support and friendship over the years.

Dr. Martin, my steadfast mentor.

All my teachers and colleagues: I have taken a bit of each of you with me in the care of my patients.

My daughter Sarah, I will always cherish your keen creativity in bringing the book cover design to life, in such a simple yet profound manner.

Clifford R. Goldstein your editorial input is much appreciated.

Most of all, God who is Master: Thank you for walking with me and for holding my hand through it all

Table Of Contents

Foreword xi
Author's Note xiii

Chapter 1
The Spectacle 1

Chapter 2
A Clear Path 9

Chapter 3
Oh Joy! 15

Chapter 4
Leaving 43

Chapter 5
Harder Than I Imagined 53

Chapter 6
Goodbye My Friend 61

Chapter 7
Asleep on the Roadside 69

Chapter 8
Not Yet, Not Now, Maybe Never 79

Chapter 9
Reinforcing the Boundaries 83

Chapter 10
No One Is Born with Knowledge 95

Chapter 11
You Don't Have What It Takes 103

Chapter 12
Not So Sure Anymore.................................. 119

Chapter 13
Deus Non Potest Percussum 135

Chapter 14
Love Never Ends...................................... 139

Chapter 15
The Interview 157

Chapter 16
Creator vs. Darwin 165

Chapter 17
My Final 30-Second Walk........................... 171

Chapter 18
The Missionary.. 179

Chapter 19
What Is One Thing You'd Do Knowing You'd Never Fail?.. 187

Chapter 20
Still Standing... 193

Epilogue 195

Foreword

Even in the Twenty-First Century, inspiration and good role models remain a great need for our youth and our community in its entirety.

How to navigate difficulties imposed by external circumstances, overcome setbacks and keep moving forward, and sidestep the quibbler is best demonstrated by someone who has truly overcome. As someone who not only understands the limitations of one's ability and circumstances, but uses said limitations to succeed, Dr. VanHorne is one such role model. Whether with a head full of scientific knowledge or in her daily work as an Internist and an Infectious Diseases Specialist, she remains true to her purpose: to make a difference, to inspire, and to rise above the mundane in service to humanity as a Medical Doctor. To do so in the face of mounting setbacks while not losing hope is soul stirring.

This book will show you how to exercise courage and perseverance when faced with challenges, faith when faced with the seemingly impossible, enduring hope when experiencing incredible loss, and admirable humility when success is achieved.

It is an honor to be a friend and colleague of Dr. VanHorne.

-Natasha Ambs, MD,
Loma Linda University, Florida State University.

Author's Note

It is my hope that after reading my memoir, one person's life will be profoundly changed for the better. It is for that one person I share my story. Through my journey toward becoming a Medical Doctor and in its day-to-day practice, every time I stand between a patient and death or face a dismal situation, I do so knowing I may win or I may lose, but I choose to stand. Sometimes, I face these situations with unease, daunted and timorous, and other times with hope and a healthy sense of "I got this one" while always praying earnestly. It is my prayer that THE LETTER will inspire a generation of dreamers to never give up, to never listen to those who, without thought, say you can't. I say you can!

Make the adjustment. Find a new strategy. Press pause if you must--then get back in the fight, and keep pressing on.

Chapter 1

The Spectacle

"No, I will not sign off on her recommendation." The tone of voice, though muted, was resolute.

"But it's customary. Every other fellow before her was given the opportunity," said another voice, sympathetic and registering unease. "Without your signature, she will not be able to take the Medical Board Exam."

"She will not be able to—," the voice confirmed without a hint of sympathy.

"Will you at least authorize the funds for a board review? Every fellow before was granted those funds, and at minimum, it will increase her chance of passing the exam."

"It will not make a difference," the voice continued. "She will not pass the exam."

The voice was that of Dr. Sanders. He was recently promoted to Professor at the Infectious Diseases Fellowship program, the highest academic achievement in the medical arena. His words carried unchallenged authority. He was notably still basking in the admiration and congratulations of his colleagues. "Hail to the Chief!" was still heard as he walked, tall and stately, through the great halls of the hospital.

In addition to his newly-minted professorship, Dr. Sanders had accumulated more than forty years of experience training doctors. This training was not only in general Internal Medicine, but he was also Program Director in the sub-specialty of Infectious Diseases. He was, therefore, uniquely positioned to render an evaluation on any doctor in training. According to his evaluation, I was not going to be allowed to take the prestigious medical boards, a decision that no one could alter.

I was tense as I stood in the hallway, listening. A feeling of disbelief overwhelmed me. It seemed like only yesterday when this very professor had chosen me as his handpicked fellow for 2010. It was he who had brought me in to join the program he led. I would carry the torch upon his retirement. But that was then.

The conversation continued after a momentary pause, and when he continued, his words were like piercing arrows landing on its target. Dr. Sanders's voice, though low pitched, was unhesitating, and devoid of kindness. None of his words carried a glimmer of hope to my listening ear.

He was talking about me, yes, except the conversation was not intended for me to hear. Searching for mental cover from its painful impact, my mind traveled back home, to where it all began.

"Diane Carol!"

Grand ma-ma calls me "Diane Carol" only when she is annoyed or getting impatient. Any other time I was "Diane." Her voice was, however, still sweet at the edges. In vain, she tried to wake me. Grabbing my blanket, she pulled firmly. I hung on tightly. A tug of war was brewing.

"Diane, time to get up. It's audition time, exam day."

The word "audition" was enough to elicit an immediate response. I groaned, half opened my eyes, and peered through my bedroom window. The soft dawn of morning was beginning to break through the dark sky. The tree branches displayed a dancing shadow on the street. I could hear the singing of a bird that welcomed the morning light. Meanwhile, in the not too far distance, a cock crowed, either begging for more sleep or calling workers to their duties for the day.

Grandma-ma was making my favorite banana bread, the sweet aroma floating in my room, beckoning me to face the day. For a brief moment, I pulled my yellow blanket, now fraying at the seams, and covered my face.

"Diane." This time her voice was sweet and pleading.

"Just five more minutes." I leaned inwardly, not to sleep, but to pray.

"Father, it's a new day, your gift to me. I love you best. You love me more…"

"Diane, I am coming with a pitcher of cold water."

The idea of being drenched with cold water when my body was still warm from the night's sleep was enough to make me leap out of bed. I headed to the closet and grabbed my slacks. They were simple, yet elegant. Most importantly, they were comfortable. I selected a matching black sweater. My curly black hair was cooperating. A dab of lip gloss and I was ready. Being pretty, I didn't need much.

I was often told that I inherited my facial features from my maternal side: high cheekbones, striking brown eyes, lips that always carry a smile, and thick long curly hair. My physique reflects more closely that of my paternal side. For that I was secretly happy. "You are beautiful. You could win any beauty contest," I was often told and believed it wholeheartedly too, until I entered Miss Montego Bay Beauty Pageant. I probably did not fare too well, as I have little memory of the contest itself or its results, except that I was not the winner.

Thinking of my parents often brought me mixed feelings. My parents parted ways while I was still too young to understand the dynamics of their fractured relationship. Mother, upon remarrying, migrated to Germany to join her new husband. The early separation, I think, interrupted the process of our mother-daughter bonding. Our relationship has always been more like a big sister and little sister, aunt and niece, and not mother and daughter. On the other hand, my dad, a police officer, was always busy. My childhood memories always place him at work, mostly nights, patrolling the streets of the dangerous city where he was assigned. I can still see him, in my mind's eye, shining his shoes until they became like mirrors, adjusting his police badge on the shoulder, and re-checking the gun on his hip before striding into the streets. He never looked back. He also remarried and moved to the city.

It was left up to my widowed grandma-ma to raise my siblings and me. Hard work, the fear of God, and the belt hanging close at hand did maintain order, quick obedience, and good manners. Our routine activities involved school, church, and home. I have no memories of movies, TV, dances, or parties, but my childhood was a happy one.

Ma-ma and I had formed an inseparable bond; I felt that she was my real mother.

Hurry!" Grandma-ma's voice interrupted my thoughts. "You're sure to arrive late unless you leave now, and I mean now," she said, raising her voice just enough to make her point.

Facing the clock on the wall, I groaned as I flew down the stairs, almost falling over Ma-ma, who was waiting at the foot of the staircase, breakfast in hand. I took a few quick sips of warm tea and a bite into her banana bread. It was more to please her; I had already lost my appetite. Grabbing the lunch bag from her out-stretched arm, I gave her a kiss on her cheek and was off.

"I will be praying," she shouted after my parting figure. "And good luck," she added before breaking out in one of her favorite hymns. I looked back, knowing that she was waiting for the final wave. I turned; there she was.

The morning wind greeted me with intensity. I breathed in deeply. The air was a bit chilly but intoxicatingly fresh. It encouraged me along as I walked briskly down the narrow and well-worn, rugged terrain to catch the public bus. And though it was five miles away, today it felt like nothing.

"Ouch!"

In my haste I banged my toe against a loose stone. Any other time or situation, I would have stopped and treated it. Not today; now was destiny time. Despite the pain from my banged-up toe, I carried on, determined. My heart fluttered wildly with great expectation. My mind was overrun with fantasies of amazing success.

If successful, I would be on my way to fulfilling my long-held cherished dream. A smile formed on my lips as my mind went into its daydreaming mode: applause from the crowd, now on their feet before me, growing louder and louder as they call for more songs!

"Ouch!"

I had another unexpected contact with my toe and a loose rock, which brought me back to reality. No longer daydreaming, I quickened my steps, faster but now more careful. The unpaved, hilly road with its deep gullies could be treacherous and unforgiving. If one were to fall, serious bodily harm, such as broken bones, would ensue. I suffered that fate at age 8 when I fell on my outstretched hand. My right wrist with its low-level pain will not let me forget. But the thought of arriving late—and missing out on this opportunity—propelled me. I pushed forward faster. It would take more than a banged-up foot to slow me down now.

A minute later and I would have missed the only public transportation heading to my destination. I rushed onto the bus, hoping I had still maintained an element of lady-likeness and grace. I quickly claimed one of the last two available seats, failing to suppress the sigh of relief that escaped my pursed lips.

The bus jerked forward, stopping at every crossroad for other passengers who were either getting on or off. There was no visible space for another body, yet the driver kept allowing additional passengers on until we were packed like sardines.

THE LETTER

At one stop, I could not help but notice a young man waiting his turn to enter. As he moved closer, he suddenly looked familiar. Where had I seen him before?

He was tall, sort of lanky but handsome. I found myself wishing that he would sit beside me. For a brief second, our eyes met. With a slight nod of the head, he took the available seat beside me, where he sat the entire hour, minding his own thoughts. I might as well have been sitting alone. I felt ignored by this stranger; it annoyed me.

Finally, having arrived at my destination, I stood up and disembarked but not without a slight glance at my neighbor, who was intently minding his own business but not looking unfriendly.

The huge Northern Caribbean University auditorium immediately overwhelmed me. I had never been in a building that big; I could not have imagined it. I came from a tiny community where the biggest building I had seen was my high school, which could not have been bigger than 1000 square feet.

This building seemed many times its size. Everyone looked so confident and well put together. I immediately felt out of place, even ill from the flood of varying emotions that were now threatening my resolve not to turn and flee. *I was born to sing. I love the stage. I will be a famous singer.* These were the thoughts that bolstered me. Only now, I was not so self-assured, and to make it worse—I was afraid. But Ma-ma would be disappointed. My nervousness and mind-bending fear could not dissolve the confidence of knowing she was praying for me. I resolved to stay.

It all began three months before when that early June, I got this long-prayed-for letter of invitation to audition for the college choir. That audition would be my stepping stone into the world of performance, my chance to be noticed and eventually perform solos and be discovered by an agent... I credited Ma-ma's faith and encouragement for carrying me that far. I would often cringe with embarrassment at her insistence that I should be chosen to sing for local plays and concerts.

"Yes, Diane has the best voice to sing for that part! Yes, I am quite sure her voice is the best suited… Also, because you have known her all your life, why choose a stranger over us?"

As I look back, I can see that those opportunities helped to cement my confidence and strengthen my talent. Those local folks were friends who allowed me to sing without fear of failure or scrutiny. This time, however, was different. These were no local folks, and they were there to render a judgment; they were there to choose. I tried to read the faces of the judges, but neither one had forgotten to wear his poker mask. They were all stone. Unsmiling. Deathly serious.

"Diane Carol!" I sat frozen. My palms were pouring sweat; my heart pounded. "Third and final call for Ms. Diane Vanhorne!"

I stumbled out of my seat towards the stage, dropping my music sheets in the process. Gathering them clumsily, I managed to drop them again, further delaying the process. I headed toward the stage, as if in a daze. The microphone at that moment chose to let out a scream, causing me to jump back before realizing that I was in no danger. I was undeniably of rural stock and therefore not fully acquainted with the workings of the microphone.

The pianist looked horrified as she struck the introduction keys for a third time. I could not find the right pitch for my song. I made a third attempt at finding the right note. It would have been hilarious if we were not all so embarrassed at the spectacle. I was rural alright; those city folks knew it too.

Chapter 2

A Clear Path

"Did today's mail arrive? Do you think that I will be chosen?" I pestered Ma-ma as if, somehow, she would know.

"Nothing yet, but be patient."

The wait was torturous. After the audition, I was told to expect a response in a week or two. Yet here I was, day three into my wait, and I was already hounding the mail. One moment, I would tell myself it was a lost cause, and the other, I was sure that I would be chosen. After all, I was pitch-perfect (though it took me three attempts!).

"Keep living." Ma-ma's voice interrupted my day dreaming. Just then, the phone rang. It was my mother inquiring about the audition.

"Did you get in?"

"Still waiting. No word yet."

I was not interested in a lecture from mom about the virtue of patience, nor did I have a desire to discuss the audition results. Mom could be quite deliberate in her chastising words, especially if she sensed my possible failure was from lack of preparation.

"Mom, I must go," I said sweetly, handing the phone to Ma-ma as I grabbed my books and started the short walk to the library.

Hours after book flipping, I exited the library in search of fresh air, water, and people to watch. But drinking water from a fountain can be an ungracious balancing act. Head bent over. Mouth hung open. Water spewing everywhere, except inside one's mouth.

"Here, let me help you," came an unexpected voice.

He carefully pressed the button, so I could focus on drinking. I glanced up into the face of my rescuer. Up close and seeing him for the second time, I could tell that he was undeniably handsome. Instead of drinking, I glanced up again and then kept staring. He smiled, and I promptly forgot the purpose of the water fountain.

How can you know so soon? That is, how can you know so soon that you are looking at the one you hope to marry?

"Are you done drinking?" the person waiting his turn asked with a hint of mockery. I stepped aside feeling a bit foolish.

"Good singing," my rescuer complimented. "I was in the audience for your audition. I love your voice. You are rather talented."

Maybe he was only being nice, but part of me believed him. I thanked him while trying to hide the broad smile working its way across my face.

"My name is Alan, or AJ, and yours is Diane Carol," he said. "I remembered from the audition." Before I could formulate a response, he added, "Nice to meet you up close, Diane Carol."

"Diane, for short," I said.

"Diane it is," he said before bidding me good day as we walked our separate ways.

He likes my singing. I smiled to myself as I walked home.

"He likes my singing, Ma-ma."

"Who does, child?"

"Never mind."

I stood nervously, peering at the carefully sealed envelope on my study desk. It read, "The University of Montemorelos School of Medicine." Inside that envelope, part of my future, my destiny was determined.

My hands trembled as I started opening the rather large white envelope. At the last minute I hesitated. What if this is another denial? I would be left with plan C.

Except I had no plan C. I fretted. It was either becoming a missionary doctor or a classical Christian singer, in that order. If this is a no, then I am done for! The week prior, I had received a letter of denial from the voice teacher, with no invitation to try again. The door was firmly shut. And now in my hand was the letter of response from my medical school application.

I could hear Ma-ma humming above the noise of her cooking (it seemed she hummed all her waking hours, and the same hymns at that). "Father, I stretch my hands to Thee, . . .No other help I know" (Wesley, 1741). It was so fitting as I stood with the letter in hand and about to learn my destiny.

I placed the unopened letter aside, feeling I needed to pray before reading its contents. Whatever the outcome, I wanted to be psychologically ready, and not fall apart, if I did not get the results I wanted. After all, I was my grand ma-ma's child. No self-respecting child of hers is allowed to abandon self-control. The expectation was to bear life's disappointment with grace. Weeping and wailing was frowned upon.

Moments later I crossed paths with Ma-ma.

"What was the school's response?" She queried.

"I have yet to open the letter."

"What are you waiting for?"

"Afraid to face reality."

At her persistence, I opened the letter.

"Dear Ms. Vanhorne: It is with great pleasure…"

"I knew it, I knew it, I knew you would get in!" she gushed without waiting for me to read further. The words with "great pleasure" were enough for her to know that I was accepted.

"Ma-ma, please don't tell anyone yet."

Too late for that as she was already marching en-route to the neighbor's house. *Let the news broadcast begin*, I thought to myself. She will get the word around before the day is through. I could not help but smile, seeing the upside: I won't have to face the follow-up questions to the news. Ma-ma would add the details as she deemed appropriate. She may have already assigned me as graduating summa cum laude.

"You have been accepted into medical school." My life had fundamentally changed by that one sentence. Its significance was not lost on me. Those closest to me were equally impacted. The process of being the FIRST of many things in my family and by extension the small community in which I lived had begun. Becoming a professional female, daring to apply for entrance into a field of higher learning, is next to blasphemy in many homes in my tiny, developing country, including mine. In my family, such a brazen thought was foreign to one's imagination. Pursuing its reality was even more a rarity.

The scariest thought was not if I were to fail. Failure would have been easier to accept. At some level, that's what was expected. The worst fear was what if I should succeed. My success could mean losing my family, to some degree becoming an outsider. There would always be that difference in the way I was treated, even if only at the subconscious level. The thought was frightening. In addition, if I succeed, the younger members of my clan would see the possibilities of the world in which they live: a chance beyond farming, milking goats and cows, gathering up chicken eggs, and slaughtering pigs. I doubt they would miss the smoke inhaled from having to prepare every meal on an outside fire pit. The thought of not having to endure such irritating knee pain, long attributed to having to walk many miles of rough, mountainous terrain with containers of water on one's head. Least missed would be getting down on hands and knees to wash and polish the unforgiving, unyielding, backbreaking, steel-like, oakwood floors. My success would mean hope even for the poor "country bumpkin," a term of intended mockery enlightened city folk reserved for the rural, uneducated poor—so subtly taught. In an odd way, I felt I was rejecting the life my family had lived for years — the life, with the best of intentions, they had offered me in return and had expected me to accept.

If I were to fail, there would be a greater reluctance in those coming behind me to venture out. They would use my failure as an excuse to continue what many generations of my family have believed and not so subtlety taught: that it was impossible to rise above one's station, that how one finishes was solely informed by his beginnings. I did not anticipate this torment. Yet I was not regretful.

I decided to remain out of sight for the remainder of the day.

Chapter 3

Oh Joy!

Days later, I was still struggling to put it all into perspective: leaving home for the first time for a new language, a new country and its idiosyncrasies. It seemed every fear and possible negative outcome paraded before me. Would I learn Spanish? Would it be adequate? Would I learn fast enough to make it through medical school? What if assimilating into a new culture proved impossible? Would I fail and be forced to return home? Scenes of the results of imagined freak accidents while abroad replayed in my mind: broken bones, robbed, lost in the city, kidnapped — on and on the negative thoughts came fast and wild. At the point of despair, I decided to call my best friend for a meeting in the park, our favorite spot.

Lucy, or Marilu as we sometimes called her, was smart, funny, and an unusually patient listener. She would refrain from speaking until the last word escaped my lips. Even then, she would wait before giving a response. Her follow-up questions were sharply focused and never rushed. She made it clear that it was my own conclusion that was important and not what she thought. Her patience and her ability to listen were skills that I long suspected she may have cemented from being a fifth-grade school teacher. In addition to her seemingly rare gift of listening, I deeply admired her God-inclined insightfulness. As a result, she was my go-to friend whenever I needed sound advice.

Moving over, she made room for me to sit on her blanket.

"So, tell me. What's the urgency of this meeting?" she asked between mouthfuls of Ma-ma's best sandwiches (the deal was I would bring her the sandwiches and she would agree to the meeting).

"I got accepted into med school."

"Should I say congratulations?" she asked, looking at me cautiously. "Last time we spoke, you were with fingers tightly crossed, giddy with excitement, about the dream life you will have as a world-famous singer."

"I do love to sing, but I was always conflicted and unsure. I want to make a positive impact in the world. I don't see how becoming a singer will make a difference in the lives of others. In addition, with all that fame and fortune to be had, I could easily lose my way."

Lucy's hazel eyes appraised me. "You take everything so seriously," she said sighing. "Are you sure about this become-a-doctor business? I've heard the training is long, arduous, and can be quite lonely."

Her expression, as she looked at me, was one of sincere concern.

"I have been praying in earnest for some time. I'm convinced this opportunity is an answered prayer."

Suddenly the mood changed to melancholy. We sat quietly. The park no longer felt fun and free. I could tell that she was thinking ahead, as was I. I would no longer be able to remain in my comfort zone; changes and sacrifice were the inescapable reality I was to face.

"Soon you will be leaving me," she said, as if to herself. She gave voice to my thoughts and melancholy. We spontaneously hugged each other.

"How about a race?" I said, an effort to brighten the moment. Before I could finish speaking, Lucy took off running, brown curly hair flying in the wind. But she was no match for my speed. I was about to overtake her when she grabbed onto my shirt. It slowed me down just enough. She took the lead and won.

"You cheat," I said, panting in annoyance while she gloated at her ill-begotten victory. "I hate to spoil your party, but the clouds are gathering. It may rain soon." The words were still warm on my lips when the first drop of rain hit my face. We bolted, running onto the well-worn path to home. All the time we were laughing and screaming in delight. By now the rain was in full shower mode, slowing our speed, but it was fun. The organic mud between our shoeless feet felt luxurious.

"Can I offer you ladies a lift out of this rain?"

I easily recognized the voice. Not waiting for a response, he left his car, umbrella in hand. He carefully ushered us out of the rain and in the comfort of his car. Lucy looked at me. Her eyes spoke volumes. "We don't take rides from strangers," they seemed to say.

"Lucy, this is AJ. AJ, this is Lucy," I said.

I hurriedly gave him the address to my house. Our eyes met. We must have looked like wild creatures. What a mess! We drove in thick silence.

"We're here," Lucy whispered, poking me in the side, as if, somehow, I needed to be told that we made it home. My home.

AJ was getting wet as he escorted Lucy to the door with admirable chivalry. While I waited, I took the opportunity to nosy around. The car was clean and neat, a book laid casually on the unoccupied seat. What is he reading? The title awakened my curiosity. It was about Luther's Theses on Grace. It was not long before I was leafing through the pages.

"Would you like to borrow it?" I was caught.

"No, thank you. I was just looking at it." Of course, I wanted to borrow his book.

"I must insist." He pressed the book into my hand.

"Thank you!" By now, the rain, as if on cue with the clap of thunder, hastened in speed and abundance. We dashed towards the house; the umbrella was pitiful in its effort to offer cover.

"Maybe you should wait a while. It's pouring."

He quickly agreed, stating that his umbrella was proving no match to the thunderous downpour. Showing AJ to the parlor, I escaped to the kitchen in search of MariLu, who was busy making tea. The sudden rain was not only coming in torrential power but had left us feeling chilled.

"Who is that handsome fella?" she asked, inquisitively furrowing her brow.

"An acquaintance," I said, my voice feigned with disinterest.

"Well, bring your acquaintance his tea and while you're at it, get to know him better," she laughed. This was too good an opening for her not to tease. If looks could kill, she would have been dead. She pretended to take cover from my glare. Approaching the parlor, tea in hand, I heard laughter. It was Ma-ma and AJ. She must have observed our arrival from her favorite spy spot and made her way down. I was hoping against hope that she would, for once, stay out of sight.

"Hi, Ma-ma, would you like me to bring you a cup of ...?"

"Come join us," she interrupted.

But I was not about to give up my escape without a fight. I knew what she was about to do. It will not be pretty. She was about to establish this person's identity and relation to me, if any.

"Lucy is by herself in the kitchen."

She waved her hand, signaling my silence. Ma-ma knows how to get her way. Even if it meant a sword fight in front of a priest, I'd better obey.

Turning her attention back to her target, she said, "So, where do you live?" "Wonderful." "And you said your family was...." "Oh, so you have an older sister, a younger brother, niece and nephew." "Ah, so you're an uncle," said Ma-ma to the obvious.

"What about you, son? What is your status?"

"Ma-ma!" I interrupted, embarrassed at her line of questioning.

"Let the old senile lady be," she said, her usual phrase for getting her way. Ma-ma was far from old age, further away from being senile, but at moments like these she will be unconvinced to the contrary, offering her supposed senility and old age as acceptable excuses for her intrusive questions.

"Ma-ma, please," my eyes pleaded. Her look rebuked me for daring to stop her mission.

"Would you not like to know?" Her attempt at whispering failed; she could be heard a mile off.

"No ma'am, yes ma'am." AJ kept up his responses. If he minded Ma-ma's intrusive questions, he was not letting on. As for Ma-ma she continued unstoppable, asking poor AJ who admirably and steadily met her gaze as she prodded into the personal details of his very existence.

"And where did you say you work?" Not once did her captive allude to his occupation or lack thereof, but that was Ma-ma's way of asking if he was being a useful member of society.

"For now, nowhere."

"Pardon me?" her disapproving tone was thinly-veiled.

"I'm in school, studying theology." AJ quickly reassured his captor.

"Theology . . . interesting."

AJ was patient and explained in great detail his line of study and the future he hoped to pursue.

Seeming to put the last piece of puzzle together, she said, "God bless you, young man. You have my blessings."

Returning her gaze back to me, "I am afraid we've left Lucy by herself far too long!" She said as if it was all my fault.

Making a hasty exit, she was gone, leaving me to face the aftermath of her doings. If only the floor would open up, I would gladly take refuge. I sat in silence, too embarrassed to speak. I wanted to apologize. I could still hear her voice like a relentless detective drilling the target. I kept my eyes fixed to the ground.

"I must apologize for Ma-ma."

THE LETTER

AJ then spoke up. "It's only right that she gets as many questions answered from a prospective suitor," he said, his voice was calm, his gaze clear.

"May I call on you sometimes?" he continued, using such beautiful old-fashioned English, but not too old for me not to understand his unexpected request for courtship.

Though surprised, I was glad for it. It was all so exciting. Since our first meeting, I felt drawn to him with awakened affection. I wanted to know him more. He seemed likable with a calm demeanor. He had demonstrated an attitude of deep respect and deference towards Ma-ma.

"I did speak of it to your Ma-ma," he informed me, sounding rather hopeful.

"You did?" Finally, I was beginning to understand her questioning.

"Your Ma-ma has invited me to church tomorrow to join in holy communion."

Just like Ma-ma, I thought to myself. So like her to want our first coming out together to be at church. She would be praying and asking God for directions. I knew her inner-workings well. I sat silently, taking it all in. He took my silence for disapproval.

"Only if you are agreeable to my request," he added quickly.

I told him I was. A look of glad relief followed. I too was feeling quite ecstatic. A date at last. Life was so wonderful!

"You can come back to earth now," Marilu's voice lured me back to the present. I was still standing at the door after AJ left.

"I want the full report," her voice was eager with excitement. There was no escaping her.

I spent most of my time in church daydreaming of love. Not agape. It was phileo. And I don't think God minded it at all. AJ entered my world a day after I ended my week of prayer and fasting. During that time, I had earnestly sought God's guidance for my life. I was happy to take the timing as divine providence.

In church, the pastor preached of God's great all-encompassing agape. I sat wondering at the idea of a mere man's response to such great love.

"It's a mystery."

The pastor's voice brought me back to the present. He was having a hard time keeping my attention. It was no fault of his. I again headed off to daydream land.

"Please rise for the benediction." Again, the speaker's voice brought me back to the present. The communion service, just like it had started, concluded with sweetness and great solemnity.

Before the last amen was silenced Ma-ma gathered her belongings and disappeared. My eyes scanned the crowd looking for her without success. There was one final location for me to look. If my search was unsuccessful, it would mean she had left for home without me. Finally, I spotted her in the dining area with friends, her plate piled high with all sorts of delicious foods. Without fail I usually joined in the after-communion potluck feast, but not this time. I had accepted AJ's invitation to the park for a picnic. I hoped, among other things, to tell him about the journey that I was about to undertake.

"Ma-ma, I am heading to the park," I said, more for a reminder as I turned to leave. Then a voice I knew all too well spoke up. It was Mrs. Rosie.

"Who is that young man with your grandchild?" she asked Ma-ma, eyeing AJ head to toe. Mrs. Rosie was known for having a deep love for gathering stories. Some called it gossip. She could spread a story in a minute.

My eyes pleaded with Ma-ma.

"A family friend," Ma-ma interjected.

But Mrs. Rosie would not be easily dissuaded. She was on a mission. Sensing a new story she was determined to get to the bottom of it and to be the first to announce it—her prize.

THE LETTER

"But who is he to your grandchild?" she continued, attempting to walk over to me….

"A family friend," Ma-ma repeated and, not to be outdone, planted herself squarely in her path. That was my cue. I took it and I hurried off.

Nearing the park, I could hear the laughter of kids mingled with that of adult voices. A duck quacked loudly in the distance. It was a beautiful day. The early summer sun was out in all its glory but was mercifully covered with some rain clouds. The cool breeze swaying made it most comfortable at over 80 degrees.

"Hi there, AJ," a voice called in a musical tone. AJ was quick to introduce me to Heather, a college companion.

"Hi," I extended my hand, but she opted out, preferring rather to look me up and down, rather disapprovingly. She turned her attention back to AJ. Lowering her voice, she muttered something having to do with Greek. I tried not to listen but was hoping to hear more of the conversation. It seemed her mission was accomplished, as she promptly took off.

"You're studying Greek?" I asked timidly, revealing my eavesdropping.

"No, just a class all theology students have to take. It can be a challenge, Greek," he said propping back on the blanket that he had carried for our comfort.

For a brief second, he closed his eyes and seemed to have momentarily drifted off to sleep. This gave me an opportunity to admire his carefully arranged wavy black hair, his strong but gentle jawline, and his neatly arranged mustache.

I was still in full observation mode when, without warning, he opened his eyes. I tried to look away; it was too late. He caught me staring. He smiled. I liked his smile.

"Are you hungry?" he asked, his gesture always attentive.

How could I be with all the butterflies that had now taken residence in my chest and were in full dance routine? He handed me his homemade jam and bread filled with all sorts of unique nuts and grains.

"I promise it is healthy," he said, "but tasty—who knows?"

But it was tasty, and when I told him so, he seemed pleased.

Majoring in theology, doing Greek, and knew how to make a wicked sandwich.

"My mom taught me," he offered, as if reading my mind. "She is a nurse but is a natural at nutrition, too," he added. "With her own little garden as proof," he continued proudly.

"Diane?"

"AJ?" We spoke up at the same time.

"You go first," I offered.

"No, you first," he insisted.

"What's your plan after graduation?" I asked.

"To be decided," he said.

I waited for him to elaborate, but when he did not, I spoke up.

"I will be leaving for medical school next summer," I said. "The first leg of my training will be in Mexico. I want to learn a second language. Spanish seems fun."

He remained silent. His expression gave nothing away. If he was disappointed about my leaving, he was not letting on.

"Let's walk a bit." He offered me his hand, helping me up to my feet. He walked towards the pond, and I followed. A few ducks and birds loitered around shamelessly waiting for food. We threw a few pieces of bread and the ducks rewarded us with loud quacks, providing a distraction from our continued silence.

"So, have you been reading the book?" he asked, breaking the uncomfortable silence

"Which book?"

"I guess not," he concluded, sounding disappointed.

"Oh, no, I mean, yes. I actually completed it two days ago."

"That was quick. Took me a week."

"I stayed up late reading. I may not have gotten the time otherwise."

"What do you think of Luther?" he asked engagingly, but I did not feel like talking about Luther's ninety-five theses relating to salvation through faith alone. I wanted to talk about my leaving, but he seemed to have no interest. I shrugged my shoulders and threw the final piece of leftovers to the ducks, who decided they were no longer interested and had taken their leave.

Just when I thought the silence was becoming uncomfortable, he spoke: "Your Ma-ma had mentioned your acceptance to medical school, and your soon departure."

I fumed inwardly. Here I was, looking for the right time, searching for the right word to break the news. I was confident AJ would be caught off guard. But I had forgotten who my grandma was. A bonafide usurper! Capable of causing endless irritation.

"Are you ready for the journey?" AJ asked in the most modulated tone I had ever heard. If he sensed my displeasure, he was not letting on.

"Sometimes yes, other times it's overwhelming. I have no idea what to expect."

"My cousin is an emergency room doctor," he said. "She may offer some perspective. I'd love to have you meet her. You can ask her all your questions."

I thanked him, promising to get back with available dates. The offer was God sent. I had a head full of curiosity and a mouth full of questions.

"So," AJ asked with intention, "why medicine?" His tone and expression made it clear it was not simply out of curiosity.

I hesitated. It's not like I had not been asked this before, but AJ's asking took on a new meaning. Should I give him the rehearsed version, the one that I made up to satisfy the curious inquirer? He eyed me patiently. I knew the answer that I should give him, but he may think me sentimentally naive. I hesitated even further.

"There," he said, as he gently brushed an unruly braid that made its way across my forehead, threatening to cover my eyes. For a very brief second, his fingers lightly touched my cheek. It felt reassuring, but it did not lessen by reluctance. I was still debating how best to respond to his question, when he decided it was time to take the walk home.

"I promised your grandmother that I would have you home by six. If we hurry, we'll get there 15 minutes before the agreed-on time."

Refusing my help, he gathered the picnic gear. We started the walk towards home.

"So why did you choose medicine?"

He seized the quietness of our walk to repeat the question. He seemed determined to get his answers. This time I was ready.

"I was about ten, at most twelve years old, and was visiting 'the Hill.' The Hill is a wild abandoned garden behind my house that has become my favorite hangout spot. That particular day I don't remember much else except that it was there that I keenly felt impressed that the work I intend to spend my life doing should make a real difference in the world. Having no idea where or how to start, I wrote a letter addressed to God, asking if he would help me to become a medical doctor. It was but a few lines on a torn piece of paper."

I sensed AJ glancing at me sideways but there was no stopping me now from telling the rest of the story.

"For starters," I continued, "the idea of me becoming a doctor was, at best, highly improbable. I hated school. Days on end of having to wake up early to take that wicked cold shower didn't help. We had no water heater. The 30-minute walk to school meant no room for a late start. I hated walking, and by the time I arrived for my first class of the day, I was already tired. I was often wishing it was already recess, even better, lunch time, better yet dismissal. The painful, long hours, of sitting and having to listen to the endless and boring classes made school unbearable. I was easily distracted and found it easier to daydream. In my daydreaming I could go anywhere, play for as long as I wanted… and there were no schools in those dreams, ever.

The worst part of the school day was math class. Somewhere, I had managed to convince myself I could not learn math. It didn't matter how well the teacher tried to explain it to me. There was no understanding it. Each and every day it was like hearing a foreign language for the first time. The teacher, in utter desperation, called me a dunce followed by quick lashes to my outstretched hands while scolding me for not trying hard enough. This made me hate math even more and by extension school itself. I finally decided that not going to school was the only solution. A battle ensued, one that I was determined to win. So for every school day there was a newly invented illness. Ma-ma would threaten to spank. She took away play time with friends. It did not in the least diminish my dislike for school. It provided no motivation to attend. In the end I informed Ma-ma that Jesus (who she said was the giver of knowledge) did not go to school, so I didn't see why I had to."

I paused for a moment to catch my breath. "Another obstacle was finances. We had no money for medical school. I knew I was in trouble when my mom asked if I expected her to rob the bank in order to pay my tuition. Mom can be very figurative in her manner of speaking; it was her way to make sure her point was clearly understood. She had no money. Student loans and getting into debt were foreign languages to us. As it was, keeping up with free education was hard enough for my family. Composition book pages were counted. Pencils were meant to last a lifetime, a pencil eraser two lifetimes. Rulers to be handed down to several generations. One pair of school shoes carried its own expectation.

It was up to the owner to make it last. Even if it came down to using the shoes only while at school itself, in the presence of the teacher. The walk to school and back home was something else entirely. Walking and playing barefooted was, for many, a reasonable option.

My family was another hindrance to higher education. Their support was a shortcoming. The long-established understanding was that females in my family stayed home to keep house, mostly with a middle school education. Usually even for those with the brightest minds and the most fervent determination for various reasons, no other options would be made available. Some of my aunts found my decision harder to accept; open chastisement was commonplace. I was often called "proud." My decision awakened unmistakable resentment. Others argued my so-called dream of going beyond middle school education was simply asking my mom to waste money that she did not have. That dream, I was told, belongs to others, folks with money for example. They promised they were being realistic and didn't want to see me hurt."

I glanced at AJ. Though he was looking straight ahead, I could tell he was listening intently. I continued, "However, once I wrote that letter to God, my thought process began to change. Oddly, wild horses could not keep me away from school. I became my teachers' best tried and true helper. I loved them and they loved me. I was on a mission. Reading was my only past time, books my daily companion. I had no better friend. There was no stopping me until I met freshman college algebra. I almost gave up, but Mrs. Williams, the Math teacher, had other plans for me. I told her countless times that I was incapable of learning math. She refused to believe me. My afternoons were spent on her patio doing math drills. It was tough. I came close to telling her to bug off. She knew it. She did not care. She had one aim; to prove I could learn math. She irritated me to no end. When I passed the final math exam, the way she responded you would have thought I had discovered the mathematical formula for landing on the moon.

Another oddity I embarked on after "my letter to God" was I took it upon myself to start visiting the local hospital, mostly to 'spy' on the sick children. I would sit, watching with wonder and a head full of questions to which I had no answers. It was there I observed and eventually met Dr. Ivan. She was a pediatrician who had escaped Cuban communism to find freedom and a new life in my country. She may have found my visits amusing. But she would occasionally stop and explain a few interesting medical facts, pointing out matching pictures of which I understood nothing. But I was not about to let her know. I am sure that the questions I asked her made no sense, but she was always kind, giving the answer to the questions that I should have asked.

It was these visits to the hospital that helped make it clear that my life was to be spent as hers, caring for the sick. Becoming a missionary doctor was now more than my calling; it was now driving me forward."

AJ listened politely but was silent throughout my entire telling.

By now, we had arrived home, he walked me to the door.

"Would you like to come in?" I offered, expecting him to say yes.

He looked at his watch. "Regrettably, I must take my leave." He extended his hand. "Thank you for accepting my invitation to the picnic." He was very formal.

A strange feeling settled in my stomach. Did I say too much? Did I turn him off?

"DC, is that you?" Ma-ma called from the kitchen.

I ignored her and instinctively walked over to the window. From there I noticed AJ sitting in his car. Did he forget something? Sensing that he was being watched, he looked up towards the window directly at me. It was too late, I could not duck away, so I just stood there and stared right back. Should I go to him?

"DC, is that you?" Ma-ma called again.

As if propelled by an involuntary will, I opened the door softly and hurried out. AJ met me halfway.

"I have a long road ahead, but will you be here when I get back… Will you wait?" Expressions, thousands of unfathomable expressions flickered in his deep brown eyes. His furrowed brow told me he was thinking.

"The letter is now a pact between you and God, and you must carry forward without the burden of a friendship left behind." His voice was kind, but final.

"Come let me walk you back." He offered.

Safely inside, I heard his quickened stride fading away.

"DC, is that you?"

I hurried toward my room. I was in no mood to face Ma-ma, yet she followed behind.

"How was the picnic?"

"It was okay. But why did you tell AJ I was leaving?"

She sat on my bed with a pensive look on her face.

"I wanted to tell him myself. I wanted to see his unguarded response to the news of my leaving." I tried to hide the annoyance I was feeling.

"It was done to protect you both."

"From what?" I could feel resentment rising. It was tiny, but there.

"From either of you over promising too early, to avoid emotions guiding important decisions and commitment." Her voice was nonjudgmental; it carried just a hint of concern.

"He is noble-minded and well-disposed towards me," I reasoned.

"But that doesn't negate his humanity."

"I love him. He's perfect, Ma-ma." Her silence propelled me to speak further. "What about me?" I asked, feeling desperate.

"What about you? Since when was life about you?"

I was upset, annoyed at her even. She knew but it didn't bother her. All she cared about was right versus wrong, determined that

THE LETTER

I learned to measure everything by God and the Bible. At times I wanted my own way, for just once to follow how I felt and act on it. Suddenly, I felt exhausted. I had no strength or wisdom to deal with Ma-ma. She would never understand, I concluded.

The weeks that followed were hard. I reassured myself, AJ was right, I should focus on my new life ahead. My heart, however, told me a different story. I did what I could and poured my energy into what was shaping up to be a difficult last year of college. Time all of a sudden seemed to be flying, and I found myself often wishing I could make it stand still. I found Jeremiah 29:11 in my memory bank. "For I know the thoughts that I think toward you, saith the Lord thoughts of peace and not of evil and to give you an expected end" (KJV). Those words helped me towards a more optimistic focus.

With plans confirmed to meet up with Lucy at the library, I placed a quick peck on Ma-ma's forehead, muttering an absent-minded goodbye. I carelessly grabbed my belongings and headed through the door, forgetting my bus fare and umbrella in the process. At the last minute, I decided to walk. The library was close enough I reasoned, but as I exited the gate, I felt a strong inclination to return for my bus pass and umbrella. I ignored the urge as the sun was out, and the day was so beautiful.

A soft breeze gently caressed my cheek as I walked. For the first time since my unhappy parting with AJ, I could hear my old carefree happiness calling. I answered and began to sing softly under my breath.

Arriving at the library, I sat in my usual spot. Twenty minutes later I was still awaiting MariLu's arrival, I was beginning to feel anxious at her lateness. Tardiness was my struggle but for her it was out of character. An hour later I gave up on her coming and decided to take a break from reading; the outside view from the library window looked inviting.

As I exited the library, I caught sight of a familiar figure whose back was turned towards me. My heart skipped; he was sitting with a group studying, likely Greek. Heather, who was doing a minor in theology, was present. I hurried outside. "Lord, help me not to feel so out of sorts!" I muttered under my breath. I felt lonely, seeing him with all his friends. They were smiling and chatting happily. If only MariLu could come to my rescue. At that moment, I found myself wishing Heather was not quite so pretty, but instead short, freckle-faced, limp hair and with missing front teeth.

Searching for the farthest corner on the library property, I sat on an empty seat. I was determined to enjoy my day, but I could not deny that seeing AJ had challenged that resolve. Feelings I thought that I had schooled away were as ever before unlearned and unruly. They came rushing back asking the same question, "Does he even like you?" as if at this stage it would have mattered. I was still brooding at the unexpected meeting when out of the corner of my eyes, I caught a glimpse of him exiting the library. His friends were in close pursuit. They looked so happy and chatty. There was no hiding. He saw me.

"Give me a minute," I overheard him say as he approached. "Hi, Diane, how are plans coming along for medical school?"

"Good, I guess." I heard myself responding. "How are you?"

"Exhausted from my studies," he responded. "This is my third and final session for the day," he continued.

"Oh," as if I care, I thought to myself. Only I did.

"What are you doing here?" he asked.

What do people do at the library? I felt like asking, wanting to make him as uncomfortable as I was feeling. Instead, "Reading" was my polite response.

THE LETTER

"I don't suppose they have already given you homework?" he jokingly asked.

"No," I said, hoping I sounded uninterested. He was trying desperately to make conversation. And I was steadfast with my one-liner responses. I had no follow up questions for him. Questions mean that one is interested, and I was determined to show him I was not. What a lie! I felt like making space so he could sit beside me on the bench. I felt like holding his hand.

His friends were ready to move on. For a brief moment, he seemed annoyed, even reluctant. I took the opportunity and quickly hurried back inside the library. Exhaling deeply, I felt like all this time that I was holding my breath. Try as I might, I could no longer concentrate on the open book before me. Gathering my belongings, I started my walk home.

"Not now," I groaned, noticing the blackened sky followed by the rumble of thunder. All too soon the torrents of rain broke in full force. The streets were rapidly filling to overflowing. By now I was not only soaked from head to toe but was shivering uncontrollably. The wind blowing against my skin was ice cold. Visibility was poor. All vehicles were either at full stand still or slowed to snail's pace. Feisty rain is customary for us islanders, but this was unusually wicked. I was no longer safe. I wavered between going back to the library or pushing forward to home.

"Gosh child, you are chilled," Ma-ma groaned the moment I stumbled inside with a tsunami like puddle of water following. She hurriedly helped me into the tub of hot water, but it was proving no match for my chilled bones. Weak and exhausted, I fell into a fitful sleep. It seems as if I were in and out of a haze for the next several days. It felt as is if I were on fire. My coughing was constant. My head was throbbing with pain, and everything around me was swaying, including the room itself. All the while a pair of hands attended me, willing me to get well.

"Diane, Diane…I think she has broken the fever." It was Ma-ma.

As my eyes became adjusted to my surrounding, I noticed AJ asleep on a cot across the room. It seemed that a lot had happened. My Bible was open beside him. It became clear. It was his voice that read my favorite Bible stories through my nightmarish dreams brought about by my illness. His were the hands that had carefully applied cold cloths to my burning forehead.

And as I watched him sleep, I found myself praying and wishing. Try as I might I could not suppress the thought. I found myself bargaining, promising to do all God asked of me if He would consider this one request. Us. AJ and I. Together. For all time and eternity. I was still conversing with God when AJ opened his eyes. The look on his face was one of relief.

He inquired if I was feeling better. I reassured him that I was. For a long while he remained on the cot. I was the sole object of his gaze. He mine. It was peaceful, like the aftermath of a huge storm. From his eyes I knew he was thinking. Intensely. As if he was putting the pieces together. As if he was deciding. I knew it was about us, and when he finally spoke, his words were far from painless.

"Diane, your time to leave us is fast approaching," he began. "I may not see you before you go, but know I will be praying for you, Godspeed." Leaning his face on mine, he lingered a second before taking his leave.

Ma-ma joined me as I watched him from the window. Even from the distance I could tell he was deep in thoughts.

"Grandma, what happened?"

"You had a bad case of the chills, fevers, and a bit of confusion."

"The sudden storm."

"Scared us a bit," she said looking forlorn.

Poor Ma-ma — the look on her face told me that she had aged from the recent event. My problems always became hers. My hurt, her pain.

"Sorry Ma-ma, I didn't mean to scare you."

THE LETTER

"AJ made it easier. He would not leave us for a second."

"Ma-ma, what am I going to do?"

"Do about what, hon?"

"About AJ, about school, about me leaving?"

Ma-ma was silent for a long time. "He loves you, but he does not want to complicate things for you."

"It has, already. I am torn."

"Let God and time do its work. It's never good to run ahead of Him. It leads only to regret."

"I am trying, Ma-ma." I replied. "But why now?" Sitting on my bed, she motioned for me to join her.

"God is omniscient," she stated. "I believe He allowed your meeting at a time of His choosing. Your lives are His to lead. Your times are in His hands." Mama answered and as expected she put God into everything...didn't matter how humanly insignificant. She gently pulled the cover over my shoulder before exiting the room, leaving me to my thoughts and the company of my cat, Jelly Bean. At times I wished I had Ma-ma's wisdom, her calm approach to everything. Not much later she could be heard in the distance singing her favorite hymns. She had managed to commit to memory almost in its entirety her church hymn book of over one hundred songs.

I was still debating how best to worm my way out of AJ's sudden unexpected dinner invitation, when Ma-ma announced his arrival. I dreaded the thought of meeting his family. I would have declined the invitation except that after much mental debate, I did not find a reasonable excuse not to accept. Excuses aside, I was excited at the surprise invitation and wondered what had brought it about. He had all but bid me a final goodbye when he departed the day before. Ma-ma was adamant in her refusal to accompany me, even though I pleaded, promising her the world.

"The invitation is yours alone." That was her final response before she launched into her usual humming, a signal that the conversation was over. I sometimes found it annoying. This was one such time.

I later watched amused as Ma-ma, who never willingly allowed outsiders near her kitchen, allowed AJ to help her once he arrived. However, I think it was just her excuse to have another chance of inquiry. After all, how many hands are needed to pour a glass of lemonade? Besides, he did not seem to mind her pestering questions. What was his favorite food? Did he like to travel? Did he like kids? And on and on. As he answered her questions, I was taking mental notes.

Finally, I heard, "Thank you for a lovely visit." AJ thanking Ma-ma was an indication he was ready to leave. "And as requested, I will have Diane home by 7 o'clock."

"Or eight," she conceded.

I eyed her suspiciously. Years of telling me I was expected to be home right after school, but for AJ eight was okay? Pretending not to see my questioning gaze, she reminded me to take a scarf.

"Take care child," she said wistfully. Her eyes softened.

I was about to remind her it was but for a few hours when it dawned on me that this may be hard for her. We have always been together. Yet here she was, somewhat handing off the guard to someone we both loved and trusted. She was being selfless. I squeezed her hand lovingly and took my leave.

There was no turning back. AJ's mother and father were walking towards us. I could see the family resemblance in his mom. Not waiting for an introduction, she smiled and said hello warmly, accepting my extended hand.

"Was AJ speeding?" she asked, trying to look stern but failed.

"No, ma'am."

"Don't cover for him," she joked. I could tell they shared a special bond.

"I heard that you're off to medical school," his dad interjected.

"In a few weeks. I hope to do missionary work after."

"Maybe you will consider starting at home? Right, son?"

"Diane should follow her plans," AJ responded rather pointedly, looking at me. It was hard to miss the slight annoyance in his voice. If the others noticed, they were not letting on. His mood had changed and did not improve as the evening aged.

On many occasions, I caught him smiling less and pensively gazing into space. Having second thoughts about the invitation? I wondered. My wondering, however, was not enough to change the pleasant welcoming atmosphere set by his family.

When the last fork was finally set aside, and with permission granted, I took the opportunity and headed towards the reading area. Rows of books awaited me. I was barely out of ear shot when I heard AJ and my name mentioned. Instinctively I halted and listened.

"...very nice, smart as well." The other agreed. "I think AJ is torn at her leaving." The conversation continued, but I quickly walked the opposite direction, embarrassed at my unintentional eavesdropping.

All too soon it was time to leave. The journey back home was furnished in silence. AJ spoke so easily with grandma, but around me silence; at times uncomfortable was the norm. We came to a stop light.

"Thank you for coming,"

"You're welcome. You have a lovely family."

"Thank you for helping Ma-ma when I was sick." I had long waited for the opportunity to thank him.

"It was easy. I was happy to help," he responded with a faint smile on his lips. The driver behind honked impatiently. The light had changed.

I suspected Ma-ma would be up waiting, Bible in her lap. And she was.

"Can I sleep in your bed tonight?" I crawled in not waiting for a response.

"Had a good time?"

"Yes, but there were times when I missed you."

"Oh," she grunted.

"His family invited me again." She remained silent.

"You okay sharing me, Ma-ma?" I asked finding her silence uncomfortable.

"One day you will leave me."

"I'll go only if you come with me." I snuggled up closer. "Am I your favorite grandchild?"

"I don't have favorites."

"Not even a tiny, tiny, tiny bit?"

"Okay, only a bit, but don't tell."

"I won't tell, and I love you the best." I curled up further, pulling the cover over my head. AJ's smile was my last thought before I fell asleep.

I woke up to the smell of Ma-ma's cornmeal pudding. Its sweet aroma was severely testing my resolve to stay true to my plans.

I wanted to spend the day lulling in nature on the Hill in prayer and fasting. I quickly collected all the essentials--water, notebook, pen, Bible, pillows, a mat for sitting and maybe sleeping--and started the short walk towards the Hill. I was swaying in lock step with the song of the sweet morning breeze. While the barely awakened sun smiled down without a hint of malice or warning of its usual noon day's wrath to come—its heat of over

THE LETTER

80 degrees; at times higher was its custom. The chirping song of the birds in the not too far distance alerted me they had long started their chorus of praise for the day. I was late. As far as they were concerned I had some catching up to do.

As I opened my prayer journal, my eyes fell on a prayer request I had journaled a few days past. It was made on behalf of Ma-ma. As I re-read its contents, I was overcome by a deep sense of sadness. I had no napkin for the tears. The hem of my skirt would have to suffice. I was on the verge of not only leaving just Ma-ma, but also the home, all I know and love. Soon the place that witnessed my birth would become the place to visit when time allowed. My home and its idiosyncrasies were to be abandoned in search of a new life, a life that may secure my never return here. The thought caused me great fear and uncertainty. Ma-ma, with the financial support of my mom, had raised me. She had poured her all into making sure that I was not only well cared for, but protected, guided and placed on the right path. She was my biggest cheerleader, always reminding me that nothing was impossible with God, and that I could do all things through His strength. A chaste godly life was the prize she pointed me to pursue.

Until now I had not realized how much she had influenced who I was becoming. She loved church. I attended all church services whether it was extremely hot, pouring rain or storming, night or day. She lived by the Bible concepts. I was not satisfied with Bible reading only but sniffing out every Bible commentary (if that were possible).

You dare to leave her? My thoughts chided me. It was quietly loud that she was already beginning to miss me. Though she tried, she was failing miserably at concealing the impact of my soon departure. It was there, for all to see in her frequent hugs, in the diligence with which she voluntarily prepared my favorite meals. She would seize on the slightest opportunities for teachable moments. On more than one occasion, I caught her misty-eyed, staring at me with her hand on her cheek. The look on her face was one of sheer bewilderment.

Am I being selfish and self-seeking? I moaned inwardly. I spent the better part of the morning thinking and praying for Ma-ma. I also prayed for guidance in my new life's endeavor. I once again recalled Jeremiah 29:11:

"For I know the thoughts that I think toward you, saith the Lord, thoughts of peace, and not of evil, to give you an expected end" (KJV).

The promise re-ignited a quiet reassurance.

I was beginning to feel the pangs of hunger. The urge for bodily rest forced me to start the walk back home. A twig of disappointment bit at my heel. I was leaving much earlier than anticipated. It had barely passed midday; my initial intent was to fast and pray up until 5 pm.

As I approached the gate, I could hear voices followed by soft laughter. She has a visitor. Good for her, I mused.

They must have been watching, waiting for me, because the moment I came into view, the door flung open and AJ came walking towards me. I was happy to see him and he me. I could tell by the smile on his lips and the demeanor of his bearing. Ever so handsome in his white shirt and blue pants, he walked endearingly toward me. Alas, if only I could run to him and hug his neck while kissing him soundly on the cheek. That would suffice. Maybe a day before our wedding. What wedding? I chided my day dreaming. I dare not hope: my life had begun an uncharted course of which its ending was no longer certain.

"Hey Diane! Here let me help you." He took my bag and umbrella. "I have been waiting all morning for you."

"Oh, I didn't know you were coming over."

"Me neither until I decided."

"Sorry we kind of missed each other."

"I had good company."

I glanced at him sideways wondering how much information Ma-ma had pulled out of him and how many of my silly embarrassing moments she had shared.

"Your Ma-ma has invited me to stay for dinner," he informed me matter-of-factly.

I was not surprised; they had developed a close friendship and genuinely seemed to enjoy each other's company and heartfelt conversation. She now called him "son."

"I hope you don't mind."

I didn't mind, only secretly wishing that I had done the inviting. I told him I didn't mind; he seemed pleased.

Hours later, with the last silverware packed away, Ma-ma quietly retreated to her rocking chair. Soon enough she could be heard humming one of her favorite hymns. If she followed her usual sequence, "What a Friend We Have in Jesus" would be followed by "The Old Correction Rugged Cross."

Without Ma-ma to keep the conversation afloat, AJ and I sat around in loud silence. It seemed like ages before he finally found his voice.

"Diane," he always managed to make my name sound more beautiful. "It's hard to put the words together. Since the first time I saw you, you have remained in my thoughts every waking hour and even when I sleep. Thoughts of you somehow manage to eclipse or usurp whatever else I am thinking." He paused, as if searching for the right word. He removed his coat and placed it around me. "I want to love and protect you by servant leadership." The symbolism of his jest was not lost on me. "Go, pursue your dreams, and when the time is right, we will continue the journey we've started."

We prayed together, recommitting our lives and future to God's keeping. The reason for his visit completed, he bade me have a good night. I then hurried towards Ma-ma's room.

"Ma-ma, he loves me, he wants me, and he will wait for me." I hugged Ma-ma.

"I share your joy but it's way past my bedtime. You need your sleep and I mine."

Sleep, though, was the last thing on my mind. Who sleeps when they are in love?

She made space for me to lie beside her, but I sweetly declined. I wanted the privacy of my room, my own bed, so I could freely re-live a million times the moments I had shared with AJ.

I reached for my diary, "Dear diary, I am beyond happy. Without a doubt, God came up with the idea of a kiss … so beautiful … indescribable … such emotions … oh to be married and soon! Oh joy!"

Chapter 4

Leaving

A sense of foreboding settled on me as I waited at the airport in Havana, Cuba.

My passport was my only form of self-identification, and it was still with the Cuban immigration authorities. It was seized, taken from me, the moment that I set foot on Cuban soil. Though I was told it would be returned in time for me to board my exit flight, those words brought me no comfort, no reassurance. I was told that it would be several hours before I could board the connecting flight to Mexico.

What if my passport was never returned? What if I were not allowed to leave? We were neighbors, Jamaica and Cuba, and I have heard enough whispered secrets of people who simply "disappeared" in the dark pit of communist Cuba never to be seen again. *Would I be one of them?* I wondered, fearfully. It did not help that there were uniformed soldiers strategically placed all over the airport, the long carbines loudly on display. I felt vulnerable and alone.

As I sat trying to make sense of the Spanish conversations swirling around me, memories of my first trip away from home began to surface. West Germany 1989. I was supposed to visit my mom and step-dad for the summer. A young teen, full of curiosity I could hardly wait to explore the new world that awaited me. However, hours after my arrival in Germany, I was placed on the first flight back to Jamaica—but not before I was held for long and tiring hours in a tiny room, my belongings thoroughly searched, and I closely questioned. My landing permit had been incorrectly filed, and that was sufficient for the young, blue-eyed, sturdy looking German who interrogated me to send me packing. But I was not about to give up my summer adventure, and so I spent the allowed time visiting the sites in England before my return home.

It was at the London Heathrow Airport that I lost my almost completed handwritten manuscript. At age fourteen, I was convinced it was to be one of, if not the best, Christian romance novel ever written. As the scenery of that long forgotten fateful journey made its way into my subconscious thought, the sense of fearful uncertainty I was feeling only increased. What was I doing in Cuba (other than, at the time, it was the most practical route to get to Mexico)? And Mexico? How would I survive and succeed without knowing how to speak, read or write in Spanish? Were all the open doors I had walked through truly of God's leading? Did I run ahead, wanting what I wanted so badly that I missed His still small voice that may have said stop?

My wonderings continued, mercilessly. I had always leaned heavily on Ma-ma's guidance for major decisions. But in this poignant crossroad of my life, she had left it all up to me to decide.

"Between you and God, you must decide. Pray much." That was her singular response.

AJ, on the other hand, was steadfast in his encouragement to go forward. Him being proud of me was heartfelt and palpable. I was provided no cover to falter. They gave me no opportunity to second guess my decision. It was full speed ahead towards medical school. I was beginning to feel weak with worried thoughts. Second guessing my decision was now in full command. And yet, amid all the angst, a tinge of excitement and hope towards the future was knocking on my heart's door. Its knock, however, was so faint, it was almost no match for the loud drum beat of fear, buts, ifs, whys, and wonderings assailing me. I tried to remain positive, by repeating Bible promises of faith I had memorized for moments just like these.

"May I sit here?" I looked up and into a pair of friendly sea blue-colored eyes that belonged to a slender middle-aged female.

"Yes, yes of course," I responded, eagerly thinking, an English speaker! Hallelujah!

She sat in the empty chair beside me, making herself comfortable and, losing no time introducing herself. She began her inquiry.

"Where are you heading?"

"Mexico."

"Vacation? Visiting friends maybe?"

"No, ma'am," I answered politely, hoping she would not pry too much. I was still feeling terribly home sick, even close to tears. My fear was that, given the right stimuli, I would start crying uncontrollably at any moment.

"No?" she peered at me waiting for elaboration. None was forthcoming. That did not discourage her. "You know, at your age, what, 15, 16?" she said, pausing as if giving me the chance to state my age. I did not so she continued:

"At your age, I got shipped off for the umpteenth time with my family to some military post. Seems registering for a new school every year was the norm. For my sister, it meant a new adventure. For me, a new heartbreak." Lowering her voice, she continued, "It was hard for me to make friends, but my dad was determined to serve his country, and mother was equally determined to support him." She paused as if reliving the feeling of the memory before continuing. "We lived by a no-excuse policy. School grades must be maintained. No quitting and always full speed ahead." From the sound of the mimicking voice I assumed it was her mom she quoted.

"Sounds hard," I said, more out of discomfort for the stranger freely revealing a painful past to a stranger she met but moments ago.

"No need to feel sorry," she said with a dismissive hand. "It made me who I am today."

Who are you? I thought. I did not have to wait long to find out; her pause was only temporary, and again her conversation quickly picked up steam.

"Now I travel all over the world as a missionary."

A missionary! She had my interest! Now it was my turn to speak; I peppered her with questions.

"Yes, yes . . . I find it very rewarding, but please do not attach too many romanticized ideas."

"Why?"

"Because it can be very heart rending"

All too soon, to my regret, her flight was announced.

"Onward and forward, Miss. No time for self-pity." She probably read my true feelings. They were all there, in my eyes for her to see. She waved a bony finger at me and disappeared out of my life.

I was sad to see her go but my spirit was lifted. "Thank you, for allowing our paths to cross," I whispered heavenward.

Eventually, after the hair-raising moments of Cuba, I boarded my flight for Mexico.

The moment I landed in Monterrey, Mexico, the capital of Nuevo León, it became clear that my life as I knew it was over. In fact, as I peered through the airplane window while it made its anxiety-provoking, up-down descent, I felt a huge lump in my throat and my eyes became saucers. There was to be comparison. The magnificent unending stretch of rolling mountains were attention grabbing. My tiny island with its customary two lane roads shouldering its small army of people would have exploded in fear at the sight of the enormity of Mexico. I later learned it was 17 times the size of my country, with 86 million more inhabitants. The extremity in the layout of the houses in the communities that were at times only separated by the turn of a corner, could not be missed. The small houses seemingly built on top of each other with their outdoor lavatories and washing hanging on lines stood in sharp contrast to the all-inclusive massive and beautiful mansions of the wealthy locals. My tiny island, I concluded, would be like half a raindrop in this vast expansive ocean. The adjustment will be monumental, I reasoned. But, I was unafraid, consumed with the thought of God as my guide. I was eager to start my new journey. My humanity prevented me from knowing what lay ahead. Otherwise I may have immediately changed course.

Exiting the airport I was instantly greeted by a chorus of Spanish-speaking voices and Mexican culture. The music, faces, language, and noises engulfed me. The smell of what I later learned was taco, the people's favorite meal, filled the air. Even a nervous gut could not suppress the instinctive flow of saliva. I was hungry. Wave after wave of mixed emotions bombarded my every move. Joy, sadness, anticipation, reservation, doubt, hope, courage all arose and came crashing in on me at once. But I had no time to sort them out. I had to keep moving. The human will to survive can be invincible, and that will in me was now in full survival mode.

Where is my luggage? I spoke no Spanish, so I had no way of asking. I decided to follow the other passengers. It worked. I found my two black suitcases, which looked battered and bruised from their journey.

Next was immigration. Once there, they made it clear that all affairs were to be conducted in Spanish. I handed over my passport. He looked at it, stamped it and handed it back, probably weary of us non-Spanish speakers. We were likely making his work twice as hard.

"Thank you," I said, but he had by now moved on to the next person waiting in line.

I exited the immigration line in search of a Miss Gonzalez, the medical school's assigned representative who would be waiting for my arrival at the airport.

"She will be holding a sign with your name written on it," I was told. My eyes strained to read the signs: Juan, Julia, Marcos, and on and on, but no Diane C. Vanhorne. She is probably late, I muttered. Confident, after a thorough search that she was not among the crowd, I seated myself on the closest bench. I smiled at the other occupant, who smiled back. A smile is truly the universal language.

Resigning myself to wait, smiling was getting harder to do. By now I had counted the 12th occupant who had shared the bench with me. The routine was becoming predictable. A new flight would arrive; minutes later the newly-landed passenger would smile at me and take a seat. They'd wait for what seemed a few seconds, and then a vehicle would pull up, resulting in an excited wave, and off they'd go. There were no signs held high with my name written on it. Of that I was sure. I was becoming convinced they may have forgotten the date of my arrival. The wrong city. The other airport hours away.

I had read through all the reading materials that I had carefully squeezed into my hand bag. I had also given a valiant attempt at reading the Spanish magazine on display throughout the airport but understood almost nothing. I resigned myself to looking at the pictures. Making matters worse I was beginning to feel the painful pangs of hunger. Fatigue, brought on by jet lag, was settling in. Hours later, I was still waiting.

I scanned around for a vending machine; a visit to the lavatory was fast becoming overdue. How would I explain what I wanted? In vain I tried but no one seemed to understand me even after diligently using my translation dictionary to piece together what I thought was a perfect Spanish sentence. The people I asked would politely smile, shake their heads from side to side, and simply move on with whatever they were doing.

At a vendor stall, I hoped for a bit more luck. "How much?" I asked the vendor, pointing at a bottle of water. She responded with what sounded like a dollar. I gave her a dollar, took my water. I tried my luck even further. "Where is the restroom?" I asked. She gave me a shy questioning look, shrugged her shoulders and carried on with her work.

A sense of frustration was beginning to overtake me. It was then that I decided to call Dr. Hill, the Dean of the School of Medicine. Dr. Hill, I was told, had done some of his schooling in the U.S. and was rumored to have a reasonably good command of the English language. The school administration had given me his cell phone as a "just in case" and for reassurance. On the first ring the call went straight to his voice mail. His greeting was not in English. I left a message, hoping that the desperation I was feeling was not evident in my voice. Desperation, worse yet frustration, cannot be the first introduction I make of myself to the dean of the medical school.

"You will easily find an English speaker to help you. English is universal." I was told in a way of easy reassurance by friends.

However, today, it seemed all the English-speaking universalists decided to avoid the airport. Everyone I spoke to responded in Spanish. I resigned myself to smile and wait. However, the bench was getting tired, and in concert with my gluteus maximus, began to rebel, sending a sudden wave of cramps down my legs, forcing me to stand up rather abruptly.

I knocked over my shoulder bag. Out of it fell a small brown paper bag. Inside was the best-looking sandwich I had ever seen, and a candy, I guess, for dessert. There also was a note, which read: "Di, if you're reading this note and hopefully eating the sandwich, it means that you have arrived at your desired destination. Whether you are delayed, and at the airport waiting, or in your dorm second guessing your decision, be assured, God never makes a mistake in the lives of His children. I am praying for you. Love. AJ."

I tore into the sandwich, praying: Thank You, Lord, for Your providence! How did I manage to smuggle a sandwich through two, rather, three airports, where my bags were fully inspected? Why, even the sniffer dog was out-matched by traveling mercies.

Deciding to save the candy for later, I all but swallowed unchewed the last remaining piece of bread. No longer hungry, the power of reasoning returned to me and I again started thinking about my situation. I must find someone who speaks English, even if it meant announcing my helpless state via megaphone.

A little later a young woman joined me on what I could safely call "my" bench.

"Hi, do you speak English?" I was afraid to hear her answer. The dreaded response, "no" was all I'd heard all day. Deep in my heart that was what I expected to hear again.

But, instead, I heard, "Yes, I am studying English at the University of Pan Am, Texas." She said it brightly and with a noticeable hint of pride. English hallelujah!

"Great, I need…" the "need" was said with emphasis, "to find the closest lavatory."

"Sure, right this way."

The corridor to the restroom was the longest corridor that I had ever walked. Once I caught sight of it, I broke out in a run, reaching my destination almost half a second too late. My rescuer was patiently waiting when I re-emerged.

"My name is Josephina," she said smiling.

"Mine is Diane. Happy to meet you." "Happy" was an understatement. This stranger standing before me was the answer to my current distress. In one breath I told her my dilemma.

"Whoa, you've been waiting for so long? You speak no Spanish but you're here to study? What will you do for language?" Are you going to be OK? Are you sure about this? The look on her face said it all and more. It was going to be, putting it mildly…challenging.

"Like you, I'll learn another language," I responded with a confidence that I didn't feel.

Her smile reflected sympathy. It was obvious she thought I was out of my depth.

"Let me see how I can help," she offered, "I'll take you where you need to be, if it comes to that. The university is close to where I live, but first let's take a look together. The school representative may be here."

I reluctantly followed her towards the rows of signs awaiting arriving passengers, convinced our efforts would be futile. I read through the names far too many times to count and each time my name was nowhere to be found. But, like a new player to the games, she was unstoppable and one by one she carefully looked through the rows of names: Maria, Juan, Cynthia, Veronica, Diana Carolina.

"Diana Carolina," she said, pointing to the sign. "I'm sure that's you." It said, "Diana Carolina de la Universidad Montemorelos."

"No, it's not," I replied. "My name is Diane Carol."

"Yes, but that's the English form." Her tone reflected her smile. "Welcome to Mexico. From now on, you will be Diana!"

Josefina approached the stranger and soon returned with documents in hand. It was a copy of the letter of acceptance the university had sent me, my picture attached. Indeed, it was Miss Gonzalez and, like me, she was waiting at the airport for the exact amount of time I had waited, except she had arrived 20 minutes early.

Chapter 5

Harder Than I Imagined

I sat, quietly, among the group of scared and nervous first year medical students. There we were burdened by the unknown, excited by the promise of the future. The commencement meeting with the dean and faculty physicians was about to begin. We were all seated up front. This seating assignment was intentional. It was to send a clear message that we were the "newbies." Without fanfare, Dr. Hill took the podium and began to speak. My translator seemed to be giving me the summary of a summary of Dr. Hill's speech, who seemed to be speaking a hundred words a second. My translator every now and again would occasionally mention a sentence, at times a mere word between long, very long pauses. He seemed keen on taking in the content of the speech for himself rather than the distraction of minding the unlearned newbie.

"Future doctors — welcome! Welcome to always being tired … still must give your best." He paused, looking out at his audience. I was straining to listen, willing myself to make sense of it. "Welcome to always living on the edge … must never fall over. Always in a hurry but must stop to listen and care. Always tired," Dr. Hill paused, at which time my translator chose to grace my eager ear with a few more sentences. "Welcome," he continued, "to the constant reminder of our humanity. Even after your best effort, patients will die. You will fail." His voice was pleasant but emotionless. The disjointed translation continued. "... Let humility guide your every care ... be not afraid to hold the hand of the dying; tears are okay. Accept failure. Be human because that's what we truly are, human."

The entire league of "newbies" sat in thick silence, listening attentively. Even with my limited understanding of Spanish, I could tell the dean's speech was of momentous importance.

"Speed and accuracy are indispensable to the medical doctor. Excuses given for its lack will never be accepted. No room for error. Every decision is of paramount importance... the urgency of every case must be assumed ... study hard ... timeliness."

At some point, the translator stopped translating leaving me to imagine the rest as he focused his attention on what the dean was saying. After the conclusion of the welcome service I stumbled out of the great auditorium onto the large university grounds. Every so often I would glance at the course outline in my hand trying to figure out where my next class for the day would be. I expected that before the day was over I would lose my way at least twice.

I settled into my new life, adjusting to its routine, in a roller coaster manner.

Some days I wanted to pack up and catch the first flight home; other days I would be quite pleased at the thought of me, the 'country bumpkin' becoming a medical doctor. "God, thank you!" I would whisper to the heavens as I walked along the campus grounds looking for the next classroom, still getting lost, though less frequently.

The more I got to know my new home, the greater the differences I noticed from my old one. There was stark contrast: English versus Spanish, one predominantly Catholic and the other Protestant. I found the many religious statues prominently displayed to be very unusual, but interesting. The evening toll of the church bells calling its worshippers sounded ominous. The locals greeted each other with a kiss on the cheek, even the newly introduced stranger like me. On the other hand, being friendly is such a big part of my culture, that a handshake, a warm smile, a look that says I see you, is customary. My island home with its sunbathed, white sandy beaches had no winter. Mexico, in contrast, had bitter cold winters, then dry, humid, sweaty, dusty, over-90-degree hot summers. Perhaps, the most noticeable difference for me was meal times. Their daily food was undeniably rich, varied, and inviting — but always served with tortilla and beans. I tried but I greatly disliked tortillas. Its aroma was enough to quiet my hunger. Rice was a rarity. In contrast for me, a dinner served without rice was seen at best incomplete and unnatural.

There were some similarities though. The one I enjoyed most was the weekend family gatherings. No books, no class, no test taking — just games and food with family — real or adopted. Not only was I accepted into many families, but God, through some amazing events directed me to my dad's great uncle's daughter, my very own great cousin, blood family. Ten years before my arrival, she had migrated to Mexico from Panama to study nursing. She later married one of the locals, a teacher, and became a permanent resident of Mexico. She was not only my go-to for all local annoyances, but became my own personal hairdresser, an understated relief.

It was all still so new and exciting. It helped that the campus was uncommonly beautiful. The university was set in a spread-out fashion and surrounded by magnificent greenery with a mountain as backdrop creating not only a scene of majestic grandeur but a feeling of peaceful assurance

There were students from every corner of the earth: from the remotest parts of Africa, to the highest points of Europe, in between and beyond. It seemed as if every culture was represented. This meeting of so many cultures and different languages helped in making the adjustment beautifully interesting. We not only better understood the what-was-I-thinking moments, but it made for a more interesting, diverse dorm life. Here we were, a group of idealists

THE LETTER

of tender age thrown together, either to sink or swim. Most of us were leaving home for the first time, unsure how best to achieve our goal. We felt both overwhelmed at the demands of our new life, and strangely unafraid of the unknown.

Making it even more fascinating was it seemed that everything on campus was shared—from toothpaste to every conversation easily overheard on the one available phone which was located to the left at the entrance of the open dorm lobby. It did not matter what time of day a call was placed. A line of students was easily in earshot of every word, eagerly anticipating their turn. I tried in every way possible to keep my conversation with Ma-ma private, covering my mouth, turning my head and my back, whispering. It was all to no avail.

"DC, I can hardly hear you! Speak up!" Ma-ma repeated for what seemed like the tenth time.

"I'm failing anatomy," I blurted out much louder than intended. Desperation had taken over. There were a few sympathetic stares; others averted their eyes, pretending not to hear, embarrassed at my plight.

Despite my doing several all-night sessions and studying to wits' end it had proven insufficient. I managed a mere "D" in my anatomy mid-quarter finals. It left me feeling acutely defeated. *I may not be as smart or able as I once believed* was a frequent pop-up thought. I expected medical school to be hard, yes, but the brightest mind, the most creative imagination could not have conjured up the actual reality. The daily marathon, the 36 hours of continuous work shift, the merging of the days into one. The disappearance of holidays. The constant onslaught of assigned homework, the never-ending lectures, the long winding projects, the interrupted sleep cycle, the forgotten meals. These things were to be accepted as normal, as the new reality.

My struggle with anatomy was worsened by my visceral reaction to cadaver dissection. The smell, the vivid imagery of cutting into the lifeless body, the pungent aroma of the formaldehyde seemed to seep in and remain in my clothing. It was intolerable. It was not uncommon for first-year medical students to enter into involuntary fasting at the introduction to cadaver dissection. I was one of them.

I was actually failing anatomy, and tipping towards failing a few other subjects. I was falling behind. How could that be? I was trying so hard, yet I was barely meeting deadlines and would have missed many except for the extensions granted. It was a hard reality to acknowledge, harder yet to accept, but I was failing. "How could you?" I asked myself. I knew that if I kept on this trajectory, my demise was certain.

I was told that Spanish was the easiest language to learn. False! I was finding its comprehension extremely challenging. But then again, there were others, like Otti from Finland. As I had done, she had arrived a few weeks ahead in the hope of getting a jump start on learning the language. And for that she was greatly rewarded. She spoke Spanish with amazing ease, leaving me to look on in wonder. I was merely figuring out how to explain A from B.

"Don't give up until the last test results are in," Ma-ma responded. If she meant to encourage me, her words fell flat. By now, others waiting to use the phone were giving me the YOUR-TIME-IS-UP look.

"I love you, Ma-ma, but I have to go."

I hurriedly hung up the phone, but not before Ma-ma shouted in haste, "Don't forget Luke 1:37: 'For with God nothing shall be impossible'" (KJV). He will help you.

Drowning in the reality of my failure, I struggled to find meaning in that verse. Shoulders hunched, I walked to my room. Though I was never bothered by the thought of quitting, I was becoming discouraged and often felt plagued by home sickness. I wished for one moment to have caught wind of Ma-ma's singing. Looking back, I often found her constant humming annoying, even mentally wishing her into silence. Only now, I longed to hear her sing the songs that perhaps would bring me reassurance. She would have encouraged me to pray, so I decided to attend Wednesday night

THE LETTER

prayer meeting and headed towards the chapel. For weeks I had abandoned attending. But not today. In the distance I noticed Martin, a second-year medical student walking towards the chapel. He was also one of the Spanish translators for anatomy class. Martin was respected by his peers for his hard work and brilliance in medicine. He was often referred to as "The Brilliant One."

"How is the first year of med school going for you?" he asked as I caught up.

"Okay, I guess."

Sensing my discouragement, he continued. "The first year is the worst. Adjusting can be incredibly difficult. You have a language barrier and there will always be that one class that will either make you or break you. You must decide which you will choose."

His choice of words irritated me.

"Choose? Who would choose to fail a class?" As far as I was concerned, the conversation was over. I conveniently walked ahead and sat in my usual seat, up front left and close to the door. It provided me with a quick exit. Martin chose a seat at the back.

The chaplain stood up, promising to need but 15 minutes of our time. True to his word, he kept his remarks brief, after which we formed a circle to conclude with prayer. When the chaplain asked if anyone needed prayer I raised my hand, requesting prayers for my studies.

"Let me know if I can be of any help," Martin offered as I whisked past him in great haste towards my dorm. I needed to get back to reviewing my anatomy notes.

"No class tomorrow, extra time to sleep in and roam the wilds," Otti announced gleefully as I entered the room. Otti was also a first-year med student. Like me, she was crazy about the outdoors, and happiest when she was out roaming freely, unhinged and unburdened by classes.

"What happened?" she asked. "You don't look too excited at the news."

"Anatomy I will be studying."

"What of our plans for hiking?"

"So sorry friend, I'm out."

"Guess I will be on my own," she lamented. "Why not pause anatomy?"

"No." Just then I was paged to head to the lobby.

"Martin is in the lobby, asking to see you."

I groaned inwardly; my legs felt heavy as I walked towards the lobby.

"Hi, again, I came to give you this. They are my summarized notes of anatomy when I took the class. Anatomy is challenging to all," he continued, "but it's one of medicine's foundations that must be mastered. You might as well face it and give her the time she demands."

"The senior speaks." I offered a halfhearted smile. "And yes, anatomy is a feat to be mastered."

"Strangely, I have been looking for these notes for quite some time and had given up, but tonight I was impressed to clean out my closet. There they were, hidden under a mountain of clothing."

"I'm severely pressed for time, and should focus on the textbook," I reasoned silently.

"I think they will help. Those notes are the final summary from the textbook itself."

He promised as if sensing my doubt.

"I'm sure," I responded with measured optimism. I was not sold on splitting my time on new information.

"I'll leave you to it," he said, shrugging his shoulders. "Have a good evening."

"Thank you senior!" I called after his departing figure. He lifted both hands over his head and shouted, without looking back.

"Get to it freshman!"

THE LETTER

"Take a look at this." I handed the newly acquired notes to Otti for her review. She was pulling a solid A in Anatomy. Her feedback would be of value.

"Whoa – this is good," she responded leafing through the notes. "No, better than good. Look at these anatomical illustrations. His drawings and outlines are masterful. Nothing less than genius. I think this will make anatomy so much easier to memorize."

I quickly recovered the anatomy notes from Otti, who was holding them too fondly and looking at them too keenly. She was not exaggerating. Only now I realized the treasure that I had been handed by Martin. He had re-written in English the huge anatomy textbook, into a summarized, simplified, easy to read, yet detailed story of the human body. With the help of these notes I was more likely to succeed in Anatomy.

"And in English!" Otti rejoiced.

I was beginning to feel hopeful by this unexpected providence. I didn't expect that quick of an answer to my prayers.

"God is awesome!" I said to Otti.

"Awesomeness?" repeated Otti in her Finnish accent. "Is that a real English word? I don't wish to be laughed at," she frowned.

"From today onward, 'awesomeness' is a word. After all, I may even be able to come biking with you tomorrow."

"God is awesomeness," Otti repeated, her Finnish accent making my newly-formed word sound even more impressive.

Chapter 6

Goodbye My Friend

Arriving minutes late, I snuck into my Embryology class in time to hear Dr. Dunn announce:

"We're all looking forward to the Christmas break, but it's not here yet." Making no effort to hide his annoyance, he continued, "Attendance has fallen significantly and quite a few are handing in homework late."

Some eyes rolled; whispers vibrated throughout the massive hall. We were halfway into our first year of training and there were already signs of fatigue, likely from the many sleepless nights. It was beginning to catch up to us. The evidence was in our tardiness, the decrease in enthusiasm and, yes, some frayed nerves.

"The majority of you are borderline passing my class. Let me strongly recommend that you stay on task and study." His caution sounded grave, a hint of warning in his voice. But the class seemed unmoved, likely a pretense.

Dr. Dunn, a plastic surgeon, was a former professor at the University of Loma Linda, California. Upon his retirement, he accepted the call to work as a missionary professor and was now teaching Embryology. He carried an open secret; he practiced what he preached. "Mr. Overdone" was the nickname that he unknowingly received from some of the students. Though his face was abnormally youthful and wrinkle-free, his gait and voice bore a much different story.

THE LETTER

"He could very well be in his hundreds," some would exaggerate. This I guess was in an attempt to keep the moments light when he piled on the pressure. This he was good at, subtle and calm, but still pressure nonetheless. That aside, there was no disputing that Dr. Dunn had the respect of all his students. He saw the practice of medicine not as a profession but as a calling. The compassionate and loving care he offered his patients had endeared him to all. His passion for medicine and his vast and impressive depth of knowledge was unbeatable. A walking textbook. The swan maker. The man who not only makes wrinkles disappear but also gifts the child born with a cleft palate the face of a goddess. "Only by following God's original design," he would caution when praise was heaped on him.

His class was my favorite, hands down. Being an English speaker, it was easier for me to master the material as his lectures were offered in English. There was no translator to mess things up. Dr. Dunn's multiplicity of emotions embodied the nature of the medicine he taught. On one hand, he could be heard in a shaky voice admonishing the doctor he now trained to, "Love your patient . . . get it right…work hard... they are here only because we are here." On the other, he would be heard bemoaning the ungratefulness of the cared for. He would often boast of the fun of medicine, we the lucky elite, and in the very next breath, it would be "Oh the futile existence of the entire medical profession." He would lament with great emotion. "Doctors are naive idealists who want to change the world but change nothing, the utter uselessness of it all," he would declare at the top of his class.

What a paradox, I thought the first time I heard his remark, which had left his medical students to surmise the possible reasons; he may have possibly experienced an all-encompassing disappointment, one said. One felt it was the memory of a patient who died who, medically-speaking, should not have. He had given all he could. Perhaps it was a diagnosis he may have missed.

Others felt he was already missing the practice of medicine; his retirement was nearing and he was grieving. He was nearing the end of his pilgrimage and was facing what comes to all—for some sooner, for others later—death.. This was a medical doctor who must have had to face and cope with depression on a daily basis or dealt with the burden of seeing the worst of humankind. This renowned doctor had alas come face to face with the nothingness of wealth, fame, position, the limits of his own humanness. Maybe, just maybe, he was staring death in the face every day. Standing before me was a man with many untold stories, and the weight of knowing that in spite of our achievements, we all eventually die had taken its toll on him.

"Many shall fail if this trend continues," Dr. Dunn bellowed into my tired brain. His piece said, with beet red face and trembling hands, he turned to his lecture.

But the mention of the Christmas break had further eroded the weak attention of many, mine included.

"Don't forget the upcoming Christmas party and there will be a surprise award," Otti whispered enticingly. "Are you going, or still being beaten by anatomy?"

"For the love of study, I won't," I mocked.

Dr. Dunn's class dragged on, and not even my love for embryology could overcome my occasional yawning. Finally, it was over. In one scoop, I gathered my belongings and headed towards the cafeteria. Tuna sandwich and a salad would do. I did not feel like having the usual Friday dinner… tortilla, and some kind of stew.

I had just settled in to my meal when I was paged to the lobby for a phone call.

A struggle ensued: Should I take the call or stay eating? AJ, or maybe Ma-ma would be one of a few people who could get me running to the phone in spite of my current state of hunger and fatigue. My heart quickened by the thought of him calling. To be told that I was loved and missed was enough encouragement. I'll

THE LETTER

go for the Bible verse of the day, I reasoned, hoping to put some spiritual context as an excuse ... although ...

My feet hastened toward the lobby. I broke out in a run. Alas, I was too late; whoever had called hung up. I turned to walk back to my room. Again, the phone rang and, again, I was paged.

My heart was filled and spilling over with deep sadness. My mind refused to accept it. It's only a dream, a very bad one at that. You will wake up soon, I told myself, and everything will be as before. After all, it was but a few days ago when we chatted happily on the phone, making plans for the upcoming Christmas holidays, when we would be together again, laughing, enjoying our friendship and love for each other.

But death is ever present. Dying is seen in the dry leaves that fall. It's there when the old, ownerless neighborhood dog, beloved and fed by all, ages and dies. I was reminded of its unwelcome, unsolicited, unwanted presence when my high school homeroom teacher Ms. Joan expired without warning. But I never thought death would be so close, until it denied me the laughter and company of someone I loved.

"I am so sorry to break the sad news," our mutual friend, Delrose, apologized into the long silence. Those in line waiting to use the phone began drifting off one by one, allowing me the space to face the news. Others stayed to offer support.

My friend, Lucy, was gone. Unlike her to run a red light, she had fallen asleep at the wheel while returning home from a teachers' conference. The days that followed were surreal. The school approved my early leave to attend MariLu's memorial service. I was offered the chance to take the end-of-year exams prior to my departure. While it was meant to prevent me from losing the entire semester, it shortened my study time by a week which is significant because of the large volume of material to cover. I decided to take the test. I must confess I did a lot of praying with symbolism. My favorite was placing my books beside me as I kneel to pray. Like me, they were under the control of the giver of all knowledge.

The ink was still drying on the test when I boarded the bus en route to McAllen, Texas, to catch my flight home. I was tortured by memories of Lucy. Memories of our last sleepovers would not let me rest. We stayed up all night looking out at the sky through her small room window. Like any youngster, the conversation was about boyfriends, dating, marriage and the holy enduring intimacy young couples get to enjoy. We were both a bit desperate. To be in our early twenties with no real suitor seemed like such a major problem to us.

"What if Paul doesn't love me in return?" Lucy had mourned. Paul was her one-sided boyfriend since he had no clue of the unrequited love she had for him. She spoke of him endlessly. If only he had known.

"Never marry any man unless God approves him, even if you were to become an old maid."

"Yep!"

"I hope we never become old maids."

"Agreed! Never to be old maids!" we laughed.

That was the last conversation we had. A gap in our weekly calls had occurred as the distance and busyness of medical school began to take its toll. Now she was gone. Her death and the way she died alarmed me. MariLu had lived all her life to please God. God's protection is infinite and all encompassing. Yet painful questioning, like the steam of hot boiling water, seeped uncontrollably into my mind. The realization that being a child of God and a devout follower did not exempt us from suffering was deeply unsettling. Grandma had taught me to trust in a God of infinite love, matchless power. That trust had been challenged. Doubt came knocking, and I was fighting back, fighting hard not to open the door to doubt.

Fear also visited and was very persistent, but I refused to let her in. Then there were my own mixed emotions. I was happy at the unexpected opportunity of seeing Ma-ma and of course AJ sooner than expected, but deeply saddened at the circumstance that brought us together again so soon.

"I'm so sorry about MariLu passing." I could hear the compassion in AJ's voice.

"She was my best friend; we talked about everything."

"I know."

"What will I do?"

"Don't lose faith."

"God was there, and it still happened. I struggle to understand. She loved God totally, lived her life for his cause. It's hard not to doubt."

"He knows our beginning, and our ending is before him."

It was hard to hear him speak of God's eternal sovereign plan. His words brought me no comfort. But knowing I was not alone made MariLu's passing and memorial service bearable. The hope of resurrection brought me a measure of comfort. I was still mourning MariLu's passing when a forwarded letter bearing the seal of my medical school arrived. I was unmotivated and had little interest in knowing the contents. A failing grade in Anatomy would not add much to my current sorrow. Success at such a moment could not be truly enjoyed or celebrated. Ma-ma opened the letter at my request.

"Seems you have successfully completed the first semester," she stated, handing me the report.

"Including Anatomy?"

"I knew you would pass," she stated.

"My story of God's modern-day miracle. During the test, I had felt that the areas I knew best were the least tested."

"That may have been the case."

"Don't be so indecisive," the professor had commented as he circled my desk, hand behind his back, eye glasses perched on the tip of his nose. He had observed me erase and change my answer to several questions far too many times. God is faithful. He shaped events and provided the aid I had desperately needed.

"A time to be happy has come to you," Ma-ma continued. "And what of the certificate?"

"Aah, inconsequential," I shrugged. "The class voted me the best shaped body," I responded feeling self-conscious. Ma-ma found it funny.

"She would have wanted you to experience the joy of your success and laugh at the silliness of the moment," she said with simplicity.

She understood. I was afraid to enjoy the moment. How could I so soon after Lucy's tragic and untimely death?

Chapter 7

Asleep on the Roadside

I was afforded little time to contemplate the changing moments of my life. Events were moving so fast that I almost missed Dr. Wade's secretary's voicemail to confirm the dates for my rotation in her pediatric surgical unit. The Bustamante children's hospital was the only one of its kind, serving the entire island of Jamaica and other neighboring Caribbean countries. As such, it was a busy site for pediatric trauma surgeries of all sorts. Some surgical events were so major it seared into the mind and left feelings imprinted on the heart that cannot be described and will never be forgotten.

The month of December seems to be the worst as the accidents both at home and on the highway seem to peak. I still have the memory of the little boy who lost his arm while riding his bicycle home from school. Trying to avoid a pothole, he had ventured too close to a moving bus. We saved his life, but he was mute for days due to the trauma of the event. I wondered at the prospect of a future for him with one limb in a country so poor in all aspects that it cannot serve its most needy and vulnerable citizens.

With all its moments of despair, I realized that even a week's rotation on the surgical unit would have exposed me to countless surgical cases that I would not readily get to experience in a more closely supervised hand-holding teaching institution, especially at such an early stage in my training. The rumor that the limitation of the island's technology and resources influenced how things were done was in fact true. Every item that could be safely reused was set aside for careful sterilization and restocking, a practice not readily seen in wealthier societies.

I was excited for the opportunity to see real surgical procedures. But, I had never seen a live brain cut open before me. My only experience of neurosurgery was based on pictures, drawings and cadaver dissection. There was one nagging fear: what if I joined the league of fainting medical students? Worse, what if I failed to maintain the contents of my stomach? This possibility was not remote. Judging from my visceral reaction to cadaver dissection the chance, though not terribly high, was at a minimum consideration.

I quickly buried the thought. I was determined to join Dr. Wade, the famed neurosurgeon, to learn every bit of knowledge that I could from him. I vowed to enter every open door and follow every lead set before me. Impressing my professors with my newly acquired knowledge was, I must confess, on my list of priorities. Upon my return to medical school I was to face cadaver dissection, part two, and I promised myself I would be ready.

Like any good student, I arrived 30 minutes early at the hospital. Dr. R. Wade was already at his desk. He was intently pouring over notes and radiological images of the patients on which he was about to operate. I felt great admiration, seeing him so intently at work. He looked fearless.

"Always learn the normal brain anatomy one hundred percent. Then you almost always will spot what's different, what's abnormal," he stated, pointing out normal tissues followed by diseased brain structures.

I looked on in awe and wondered at the magnificently created brain before me. Coming at me at once from all angles was the vast information I needed to digest. I felt like a child wearing sandals and a T-shirt being asked to climb Mount Everest in the winter. I remained silent the entire time, trying my hardest to stay focused and not to get overwhelmed regarding the intricacies of the complex yet fragile structure of the human brain, no cell out of line unless diseased. *Lord, does Dr. Wade, let alone anyone, truly understand it?* I found myself thinking in wide-eyed awe of all of it.

"This will be our first case," he said pointing to a glioblastoma tumor on the brain of a 7-year-old boy. "He had his first seizure before he could walk." I followed the pointer trying to put the pieces together. My recent exposure to anatomy and cadaver dissection was helping me to make some sense of it, but there was so much to learn!

"Ready?"

"Ready."

"Come. Let's go!"

With that he stood up abruptly, heading straight to the operating theater, a trembling medical student following closely behind.

Cutting into a child's brain was not easy. I was surprised to see the amount of bleeding that occurred after each incision. As fast as the neurosurgeon assistant cauterized and mopped up a bleeding vessel, another site would start bleeding.

Lord, what did I get myself into? My stomach was churning. Dr. Wade was again in one of his long silent moods. The operating room was eerily quiet. His eyes were flickering rapidly up and down, side to side. The furrowing of his brow reflected the intense brain work that was going on behind his pale brown eyes. These periods of intense silence often signaled three possibilities; complications, findings more worrisome than expected, or just sheer fatigue. Such times, no one dared interrupt his non-verbal request for silence. I was nervous to the point of feeling afraid to look. "Please, God, guide his hands," I prayed silently. My feet were numb and heavy from just standing, observing, but my adrenaline had kicked in, keeping me alert.

Finally, Dr. Wade broke the silence with the welcome words, "We're done." A sigh of relief echoed throughout the room. The patient was quickly whisked away to the surgical ICU for continued care and recovery. It was now time to update loved ones who were no doubt anxiously waiting. I imagined dads pacing the halls, the moms clutching their hand bags and quietly praying.

Many people greeted Dr. Wade as we walked along the long hospital corridor to the waiting room. A few colleagues nodded in respect; others asked for details of the surgery.

"This is sometimes the hardest part of my day," he said as we walked, talking as if to himself. "That is, the time to face their families."

I watched as he struggled to find the right words as he discussed the outcome and possible complications and the road ahead.

"The surgery was successfully completed, but the boy risks swelling to the brain and possible neurological damage," he explained to a worried parent's question.

Though his conversation remained kind, with a demeanor of compassion, he gave a realistic assessment without offering false hope. I was observing and taking mental notes. I, the understudy, would one day do the same.

The sun had long bid farewell when we finally exited the hospital and headed to the car for home. Using the phrase "bone weary" to describe how I was feeling would be an understatement. I dreaded the 35-minute drive home. The day's events had taken its toll. Dr. Wade only took a 30-minutes break for lunch. But even while we ate, he had reviewed and discussed the postoperative CT brain with the radiologist. In reality he had worked through the entire 30 minutes of our presumed break. I noticed him downing the last bite of his sandwich as he headed to the lavatory. He modeled with perfection what eating-on-the-run looked like.

By the time the last surgical sutures were drawn and knotted my eyes were heavy with sleep, and my reflexes were those of a drunk. I found myself debating whether I should take a quick 10-minute rest before I entered the highway, or just push on home. The thought of a warm bath and bed awaiting propelled me forward. I put my head on the steering wheel briefly…

The next thing I knew, I woke up, startled by a tap on my window. As my eyes adjusted to my surroundings, I saw AJ's face at my window, motioning for me to unlock the door.

"Are you okay?" His tone was clearly worried.

I nodded. "I am okay."

"Do you know what time it is?"

Before I could formulate the thought, he answered his own question. It took me a while to realize that I had fallen asleep at the wheel. It had caused a stir when I did not return home at the expected time. When all my pages went unanswered they had imagined the worst had befallen me. I sat feeling self-consciously foolish.

"Long day eh?"

"That would be an understatement. It was long and arduous. No rest between cases, and Dr. Wade's incessant teaching. His voice is still in my ears; the experience was close to overwhelming."

"I can't imagine it," he sympathized, "but promise next time you'll choose safety over the expediency of driving home."

"I was overtaken by sleep. I just wanted to get home."

"Promise me," he insisted. "I imagined the worst. We just lost Lucy."

"I promise."

No longer feeling tired, much less sleepy, AJ and I decided to idle the remaining hours together. In truth, since my early return for Lucy's memorial service and Christmas break we did not get a chance to really hang out together, alone.

Looking through family albums and talking sounded fantastic. I agreed to his offer.

It was unlike him to share about his life, less so his extended family. Initially, I was a bit apprehensive that he would at any moment recover his senses and stop sharing so much. He did not and I was glad for it. While he spoke, I could not help but wonder if the day's events were divinely guided, and that, perhaps, the day was truly meant to culminate like this: with more bonds of love and affection forming between us. I had gained more insight into who he was in a few hours than the two years since we met. His focus. His ideas. His thoughts. His laughter. His silence — all there for me to take in, enjoy, pack in my memory bank to later relive.

In a beautiful, engaging manner, he shared with me the process of his decision to become a theologian. Without doubt he felt called to his chosen profession. It was clear he believed becoming a pastor was God's purpose for his life.

He intended to do it wholeheartedly. He sounded resolute. He would not count the cost. He felt no cost was too great.

Hours later, thanking AJ for his hospitality, I announced my departure.

"I'd love to accompany you home, but was advised to the contrary."

"Ma-ma's request?"

"Yes, things must not only be done right, but must also look right," he mimicked.

"Yes, sounds like Ma-ma alright." I responded, waving goodbye.

Ma-ma was likely afraid of Ms. Vick, our neighbor observing my return from her spy spot–the tiny curtain opening by her window where she positioned herself daily to observe the world's happenings. No doubt she saw when I left home the day before, only to return the next morning accompanied by AJ; imagine the tale to be spun! Unimaginable!

There are many joys living in small communities; we become our brothers' keepers, but it has its downsides. Gossip. Stories spread like wildfire. Whether they were true or false did not make a difference. And in my tiny religious community it took very little to be labeled an outcast. Its validity mattered not. At moments like these, I appreciated Ma-ma's insight and actions taken to protect me, and by extension AJ's reputation.

ASLEEP ON THE ROADSIDE

Ma-ma was outside pulling weeds from her poorly designed garden when I arrived. "Look who decided to come home," she muttered.

"I missed you too, Gran. Sorry for causing you to worry. I was just so sleepy." I hugged her good morning. She didn't return my hug, clearly upset with me.

"How was your time with Dr. Wade" she asked. I recognized the tone of her voice and I knew what it meant. She was more than upset, but highly displeased.

"Great, he's the best, " I boasted and described, in great detail, his surgical skills. I was careful not to leave out the pride and admiration it evoked in me.

"It seems all that matters to you of late are grades, influence, and colleagues who you consider to be of outstanding talent."

I opened my mouth to defend myself, but quickly reconsidered. Her tone of voice and stern look sounded warning bells.

"They tend to have your full attention, not to mention your glad admiration. I can't imagine how you'll be once you're full into this doctoring thing. Soon I will be of little influence," she continued, but the last sentence was said as if to herself.

I found her comment singularly out of character, even painful. She herself was a high achiever in her own right. It didn't matter that she taught herself to read at an early age by reading the Bible. It was clear that my unintentional night out had displeased her. Was a row between us brewing? I never won when we argued. I decided to take cover. Why start a war you know you'll lose?

"I will be in my room if you need me." I hurried off before she could stop me.

Upon entering my bedroom, I determinedly closed its knob; it was not with malice, yet I felt more than a tinge of guilt in doing so, as it meant do not disturb; stay out. I had just returned to Ma-ma for a short stay. I could tell she needed my company, but I was changing. She stated I had outgrown her, a claim I vehemently denied. However, emotionally and in order to survive I needed at minimum some moments alone. Dorm life at school did not only present a world of swift permanent changes, but it also meant the idea of privacy became a thing of the past. No escaping to one's room for a moment of solitude, not when it's shared with as many as two other students of totally different personalities. Imagine the incessant extrovert with the bone-chilled melancholy, or the early sleeper with the night owl shuffling about the room. The neat and tidy with the disorganized who could not remember the last place a shoe was seen.

Hours later, I was still shut up in my room moping, wishing I could have it all ... my chosen career, my work, a life with AJ ... now, at once without all the struggle. When I heard Ma-ma's footsteps coming up the stairs, I wished her away. They hesitated at my door. I imagined her standing there with her raised hand. Staring at the door, I waited for her to knock. Her footsteps sounded lonely as they disappeared back downstairs.

Poor Ma-ma, I thought, twice a widow, she buried two of her young children, yet she carried on as if unscathed. Never a complaint or lament. In fact, I have no memory of her speaking of the two husbands she buried nor her two daughters that were placed in an early grave. Never a note of self-pity escaped her lips.

Though I loved her dearly and admired her to boot, we did not always see eye-to-eye. Still I accepted her guidance and, in many ways, yearned to be like her. Strong, fearless, passionate in her endeavors to be Christlike. "Don't be afraid," she would often tell me, you are more capable than you think; but today I was sure I was not capable. I felt lost, afraid, and in grief over Lucy's untimely death. Afraid that I may not be enough for the road ahead. Afraid of life choices and its consequences. Afraid of the changes–afraid of having to once again leave my two great loves behind, her and AJ.

"Oh, Lord, our help in ages past, my hope for years to come" (Watts, 1719). Yep, there she was again, singing her usual hymns. I could hear her singing above the chattering noise of pots and pans in the kitchen.

So timely was her choice of song. I reached for my Bible, my childhood companion. No other book I love better but, of late, in my rush of life, it was often ignored. Sitting on the bedside table, it looked quite lonely. The dust on its cover tells the story of being ignored for far too long. We have not had a heart-to-heart visit for a while.

"Thou wilt keep him in perfect peace, whose mind is stayed on thee; because he trusteth in thee" (Isaiah 26:3 KJV).

I read with my eyes, but my mind was elsewhere. Inwardly, I felt off balance, adrift. I had experienced so many changes in such a short time. I was struggling to put them all into perspective.

"Oh, Lord, please help me. My faith is weak. I am fearful," I prayed. Desperate short prayers had become part of my routine.

Chapter 8

Not Yet, Not Now, Maybe Never

"Your mom called to say she is at the airport," Ma-ma informed me the second that I emerged from my room.

"Now? Why the surprise visit?"

"Try not to look so distressed — nothing to be done — she is here. In a few hours, AJ and your mom will be facing each other." Grandma's tone of voice was matter-of-fact, telling me she was downplaying the anxiety my mom's, her daughter's, surprise visit was causing. If asked to use one word to describe my mother, it would be a tornado.

"Wild horses will not keep her away…for this. And rightly so," she continued.

I groaned inwardly; mom must have gotten word of my dating. Her coming was most likely to investigate the seriousness of the situation. It mattered little that I was not ready for the big reveal and the inevitable meeting. Our relationship was still developing. If she disapproved, she would be incapable of saying otherwise. She would be blunt and could be scornful. If need be she would work to see sabotage of our relationship. AJ's chosen career for her would be a non-starter. Naturally, she had a preference for a life of ease and comfort, and yes, she would not mind having some influence based on a decent bank account – a position she craved not only for herself but her children. The work of a pastor held no promise of that.

THE LETTER

Shortly after her arrival, my mom met with AJ. I was happy to sit in a corner as they held court, speaking in hushed tones. In vain, I strained to hear their conversation. Mom's expression was pleasant enough but, knowing my mom, it didn't mean that he had her approval. "I may need to intervene and rescue him," I mused. Mom could be an engaging conversationalist, yet fiercely disagreeable. Tactfulness was not one of her strengths, unless it was to her benefit.

I decided against intervening. It was vital that they both got to know each other. I was relieved when the meeting was over. She was courteous as she bid AJ goodbye.

"I hope you're not planning a life with this young man," was mom's first rebuke once AJ was out of earshot. "At best boredom and hardship is all I see here," she cautioned.

"Boredom?"

"I can't see how sitting in a church, hat on your head, dressed like an old maid with ten kids appeals to you!"

"How about nine instead, no hat, and a seat at the back?" My joke fell flat. Her withering look indicated disapproval.

"Diane, can you put a camel through a keyhole?" Mom asked out of the blue. We were at the airport waiting for her flight back to Germany.

"No, Mom," I placed an emphasis on the "no," feeling that was definitely an eye-rolling question.

"Except that you can. Indeed you can," she responded with earnestness in her voice.

"Really, Mom?" I laughed, thinking she was up to one of her usual funny stories, but her demeanor was sober.

"You just have to find a way. You may have to kill the camel, burn it, get a straw, gather the ash, and blow it through the keyhole," she explained in great detail. Pausing, she leveled a steady gaze. "There is always a way to achieve what's worthwhile. You just have to find it."

"Good luck in school," she added almost like an afterthought.

She knew that I did not believe in luck — just God and hard work.

"I know that I am gone all the time, but I love you no less." Her expression was wistfully melancholy. Her hand was on my shoulder.

I knew she loved me, and I her. I hoped she knew, but just in case, I said, "I love you" back with emphasis.

We said our goodbyes and she hurried towards the airline check-in counter. At the last minute she hurried back over and said with great affection, "I like AJ. He is a great guy. You should marry him, but finish medical school first. Don't forget your promise."

Before I could recover, she had already disappeared in the departure line to Germany.

Chapter 9

Reinforcing the Boundaries

I wished that I had not promised mom I would spend the entire weekend with Granny Lita, my dad's mom, but I had not seen her for quite a few months. So, mom insisted I visit before I returned to medical school.

Spending time with Granny Lita was always fun. Her cooking was fantastic.

She would always sit and talk with me, showing great interest in whatever was going on in my life, answering the questions that Ma-ma would not entertain about male and female issues. She often told me I was thoroughly beautiful. I loved hearing those words to describe me. Because of her, I concluded that I was created just before God rested on the Sabbath. He knew that He was about to rest, so it didn't matter that I asked Him to add a few extra bits of beautification for me.

While I was happy to spend time with Granny Lita, my heart was not with her. It was elsewhere. I could not muster the courage to tell her that I wanted to leave early, so I decided to settle in.

"Why don't you go take a walk on the beach. It may do you some good," she suggested. "After all, it's such a beautiful day, and it may settle your mind."

Needing no further encouragement, I headed towards the beach. It was hard to find an islander who did not love the beach and believe they were literally born on its shores. Yet few bothered learning to swim, me included.

Arriving at the beach, I made myself comfortable on its sand. My sandcastle was coming along nicely, and my mind was beginning to feel at ease when I heard my name called. It was Zac Miller, who was now walking towards me, in haste, a big grin on his face. He and I had gone to high school together, sat in the same classes, and were friends but had lost contact upon graduation. Looking at him he had not changed much. I was curious to learn if his attitude and arguments remained the same, too.

"What are you doing here?" he asked, plopping down beside me without an invite.

"Visiting Granny."

"How are you doing? What's new?"

"Nothing's new. Just building a castle in the sand."

"Since when is going off to medical school nothing?"

"Oh, that?"

"By the way, congratulations." I eyed him puzzled. "Your granny said you will be getting married any day."

I could not help but smile; she filled in the dots to her liking. She must have caught word of AJ's and my growing friendship and that was enough for her to set the wedding date.

"I hope she will inform me of the date and location so I could, at minimum, making a showing," I quipped.

By the time Zac stopped laughing, I was convinced that I could make my name in comedy. We sat around making small talk, followed by long silences, each unsure how to carry the conversation. In truth, I was looking for an opening to witness. I decided to tread carefully. The mention of anything remotely Bible-related was enough to send Zac running, leaving a cloud of dust to tell the tale of his quick escape. I tried so hard while in high school. Like every other girl, I had a massive crush on him. We all thought he was very handsome, well-articulated, brilliant, a talented athlete, and easy going. But he was "unchurched and secular," and per Ma-ma he would never do, so in my simplicity I set out to convert Zac for myself. Over time, as I matured, I began to see the situation less selfishly.

Let's see how fast he will run this time, I thought to myself. "Zac, I may not see you again or for a long while, so can we continue our old high school discussions?"

"Oh, boy, here it comes," he groaned. "The ones about trying to gain the world at the expense of losing out on what truly matters, whatever that means."

"Instead of just following our own ambition, imagine if we do it for the greater good of humanity and to honor God …"

He shifted nervously.

"Isn't that what we all do, work on fulfilling our dreams and ambitions?" He sounded a bit incredulous at the suggestion to the contrary.

"I hope I am not sounding way out there, or more bluntly, you won't think I am being goody-goody, but I think we were created for so much more."

Zac was quiet as I told him about the different worldview as I understood it and how we all have to choose: creation vs. evolution, resurrection vs. eternal loss, good vs. evil. It was awkward, but I felt this may be the last time that I would have this kind of conversation. He might have been less willing to listen once he achieved whatever it was he was pursuing, I reasoned.

It was clear he was destined for big things. He was voted most likely to succeed his final year of high school and by all accounts he was on his way to make it happen.

To my relief, he listened to it all and I was a bit surprised when he asked, "Is that why you are becoming a doctor? You've always been kind of different. What's with you?"

"Can I be honest?" He arched his eyebrow. "You are the only person I'll ever tell this. This is a high secret," I joked.

THE LETTER

"I can keep a secret," he laughed.

"I once wanted to be a girl evangelist."

"Really?" he mocked as if surprised. "You, an evangelist?"

"Yes, really."

"And what happened?"

"God led me to a different path."

"To be a doctor?"

"Seems so."

"To be honest, DC, you make life sound so interesting, so easy," he said after a long pause."

"A matter of choice," I simplified.

"I appreciate the conversation, but I don't know. I am not sure."

I was still sitting where Zac left me, pondering what I could have said differently. I wanted him to experience what it was like to have a heart with a desire only for the good, the uncommon, to live a life unburdened by selfishness, to spend every day giving of oneself. I didn't know that life fully, but every day I caught glimpses of it in Ma-ma. She was simple, happy, giving, selfless, unburdened by the fleeting foolishness of humanity – "a God-led life" as she called it.

Oblivious to the waves that were beginning to move closer to shore, I soon realized that I needed to either move along or remain seated and get wet. Not missing a beat, I continued building my sandcastle, daring the waves to topple over the castle that I had carefully built. Without warning, she rushed in and carried off my castle. Just like that, it disappeared without a trace. It didn't matter that it took me the better half of the morning to build. I felt a tinge of annoyance.

"May I join you?"

The voice was so easily recognizable. Without waiting for a response, AJ sat down close enough to be acknowledged, but with enough distance so we could look at each other while we spoke. The world for me was all sunshine again. *Oh, life is so good for me right now*, I thought to myself.

"Diane, I miss not having you around."

I hoped I was successful in hiding how happy hearing such a declaration made me feel. Every human should have the opportunity to thoroughly, helplessly, fall in love at least once in their lifetime.

"During our process of courtship there are physical boundaries that I hope never to cross," AJ continued rather solemnly. I could tell that he was choosing his words ever so carefully.

I knew exactly what he meant. My head, my upbringing in a conservative Christian home and my own personal decision all said the same: "Wait." We chose chastity.

"We agreed on those boundaries a while back, no playing around the edges," I responded.

"It's not always easy to maintain focus on our pledge when I am around you."

"I share the sentiment, but isn't that how the Creator intended us to be ... totally and honestly attracted to one's soon-to-be spouse?"

"Nothing has changed, but I have to be honest in facing my own humanity." Silence followed. "You and your Ma-ma have placed a trust in me that I cannot take lightly."

I was beginning to understand why my phone calls went unanswered for days, why he had placed an obvious distance between us. He was struggling.

There was another concern. Since meeting AJ, I got the sense my comings and goings were more scrutinized, my times more closely accounted for, so I asked, "Did Ma-ma lecture you about us?"

"No, but I needed time away to reaffirm the strength and reassess the boundaries of our relationship. I want our courtship to honor God in all. Old-fashioned maybe," he stated in his usual melancholic sort of way. He continued, "Still there are times that I feel unsure. My inner thoughts and feelings disagree. I want you to feel protected and honored around me."

"Is there anything you want me to do differently?" I asked.

"Short of covering from head to toe, nothing really," he humored.

THE LETTER

A long silence followed but I was beginning to understand more clearly. Ma-ma had glossed over so much. Topics of certain human emotions, given by God himself, were off limits for discussion as far as she was concerned. "Wait for marriage," was her total input. "Protect your land, and don't give away what you can't take back," was her very colloquial warning. It was enough. I understood.

I myself made promises, chastity included, that I intended to keep, but now the proverbial rubber had hit the road, and here was someone who was willing to guard our relationship, even when it was at times seemingly more difficult for him. His intentions toward me were undoubtedly selfless, uncommonly noble. He was willing to take steps to safeguard our mutual pledge to wait until marriage.

"We'll keep our pledge with divine help and wisdom," I reassured.

"Not trusting self."

"We'll reinforce the boundaries."

"Option of chaperone?"

"We'll be okay."

"We'll be okay."

"Settled?"

"Settled. Am I forgiven for not answering your calls?"

"You mean for running off? Yes, I'll forgive you, but on two conditions."

"What are they?"

"First, you race me to my Granny Lita's house, and the other I'll tell you if I win." (There is something unexplainable about us island people and our love for racing. And in everyone's mind they have champion potential. No coincidence we boast Usain Bolt.)

"You'll tell me if you win? Sounds like I'll have to let you win."

"Ya, if you want to know."

"That's a race to lose. Either way, I don't have running shoes. You have the advantage, so …"

I took off running before he completed talking; however, I was easily overtaken.

"Ouch, my foot hurts!" I limped. AJ stopped long enough to assist, but I was off and running before he realized my trick. But, again, I was easily overtaken.

"Help!" This time, I was on the ground.

"Can you stand?" he asked, helping me to my feet. I took off running before he could find his balance.

"I won!" I shouted as we got to Granny's place.

"That doesn't count!" he protested.

"I see that you found her," said Granny, smiling and shaking her head in disbelief at the spectacle.

"I did, Ma'am," AJ answered.

"I didn't know that I was lost."

"By the way, I'm here to take you home at your Ma-ma's request."

"Okay, then let me fetch my belongings." I was secretly so happy.

"So, what was the other condition now that you won?" he asked as we climbed into the car.

"I have seven days before I go back to school, so I was wondering if we could spend them together?"

"All seven days?" he repeated followed by silence.

"Every day."

I waited, patiently on the surface, but I was squirming in apprehension on the inside. Finally, he responded, "It's my week to be out in the field conducting evangelistic seminars. But, if it were possible, what would we do?"

"I could help with the paperwork. I will make a good usher, or I can sit in a corner and listen and learn just what it is that a theologian in training does."

"The work is all consuming, and there are no roads for vehicles to reach where I go. It's all on foot, a lot of walking in the sun."

"I love to walk. I was born in the sun, and hard work and I are friends."

He seemed to like my answer; his eyes brightened, lips smiling. "We could start early." He was already planning ahead.

"At the break of dawn."

"I could join you and your Ma-ma on time for morning devotion."

"You'll love her breakfast."

We drove the remaining distance, fingers intertwined. It seemed we both forgot how to stop smiling. The most perfect day ever to be granted to our island was gifted to us that day. The sun was on its best behavior unlike its usual 90 plus degree heat wave. The ocean view was pristine and calm. The coolest most comfortable breeze was ours to enjoy, and the trees on the roadside danced in synchronized order. To be in love . . . such joy!

Arriving home, I updated Ma-ma about my visit with her sister and my meeting Zac Miller. He was her former Sabbath school student.

"Intelligent young man. "I am glad you got to speak. The seed of faith has been planted, and it will grow," she confidently remarked. But I was still hanging around her, my cue, something else was afoot. I just wasn't sure how to break the news. My "week plans" with AJ were spontaneous. I hadn't taken the time to consider her input. She may find my idea preposterous, outrageously inappropriate even.

"What's on your mind?" Ma-ma asked, a tinge of impatience in her voice. Once I revealed my upcoming week's plan, she sighed. "AJ has already sought my advice and permission. I told him it was okay."

"Thank you, Ma-ma!" I hugged her, relieved, trying to hide how elated I was.

"Tomorrow he will bring you his plan for the week."

"It's all done. It seems that you are spending the week with his mom and dad."

"I am?"

"It's all arranged."

"It is?"

"Yes. He'll be staying next door with his "spiritual mom and dad," the Knights, who were instrumental in leading AJ to Christ. He credited their influence and encouragement for guiding his decision to become a theologian.

I was silent, but my mind was working overtime. An entire week with his parents? The pressure was on.

"Time and closeness to know each other," Ma-ma reflected aloud.

"She'll watch me."

"You'll watch her."

"A week with his parents was not part of my original plan."

"Maybe this is his way of getting his parents' approval?"

"What if his mom after watching does not approve of me?"

"Then both of you will have the first real test to your relationship."

"Ma-ma, can I back out?"

Silence.

"Ma-ma!"

"Ah, child, we never know where spontaneity will lead."

"Help me back out," I pleaded, but as expected Ma-ma was already off and humming.

I sat by my bedroom window, patiently watching and waiting for AJ's arrival.

As was his custom, he arrived early, and today was his earliest yet — a good twenty minutes at minimum. He parked and waited; ever so often he would glance at his watch and look up toward my window. I had the advantage, as I watched undetected. As if to check his appearance, he peered in the mirror before alighting from his car and hastily walked toward his desired destination … me.

I was warned against rushing outside to meet him in an undignified manner. "Wait inside," Ma-ma requested. I would have run out to meet him anyway, except she was hovering close by in the kitchen.

Ding Dong!

With great restraint, I waited.

THE LETTER

Ding Dong! Ding Dong! More urgency to the doorbell. Ma-ma stuck her head out from the kitchen. Her look said it all.

"You asked me to be patient." I feigned naiveté and walked slowly toward the door, but I was running on the inside.

"Ready?" His eyes said it all. My joy matched his.

He handed me a bag. Inside was a book. He knew I was a consummate book lover. The title was *How to Talk so Your Mate Will Listen and Listen so Your Mate Will Talk* (Van Pelt, 1989). I found it interesting.

"Don't stay up all night reading, and no rush. You have a week. We can talk about it together when you're done."

"Let's go then."

"Let's go."

"Did you have breakfast?"

"No, I wasn't hungry. Did you?"

"No, I wasn't either. Did you sleep?"

"A wink. How about you?"

"A little."

"I love you,"

"I love you more."

He offered me his hand. I held it. We started our week's journey.

As AJ and I drove to the airport, I gave my heart permission to fully experience the emotion of saying goodbye, again. I could see the airport tower coming into view. It stood like a painful haunting signal of our soon-to-be separation. Coals of fire were in my chest. The recent week that we shared together in the "mission field" served not only to bond us closer in heart, but also painted a clearer view of what my role as a missionary doctor joined with that of a theologian would look like: a life of constant service to others, and one of simplicity.

His work mirrored what I hoped to do in the future. To share that future with him was now my ultimate goal. I was convinced I wanted to spend the rest of my life with no one else. He was uncommonly kind, and keenly sensible in every way possible — sincere and steadfast in doing the right thing even when unnoticed. I was an admirer of his devotion and love for God, impressed by the many ways he shared in the sadness of strangers, and his faithful prayers for the sick and bereaved. He did his work with genuine compassion, and when he preached, others listened. His words inspired people to want God. His only fault? He was moody, contemplative to the point of deep melancholy. He could sit in contemplation for hours without a word passing between us.

"Don't fret," he said, as if sensing my anguish. His words brought me closer to tears.

What will a future together be like? I silently wondered. "We are destined to be poor," was his response to my thoughts.

"But happy."

"I know."

"We will share everything, no secrets."

"Yes, everything."

"I will get your lunch bag ready."

"Like you've always done."

"I can't iron. Will you iron?"

"Yes, my mom made sure that my brother and I learned."

"I promise not to nag."

"I will be kind."

"I will learn to cook."

"I'll help, too," he said.

"Our journey will be uncommon, less likely to be easy."

"I'll understand. I'll love you still."

I reached over and held his hand. He held mine back, tightly. We arrived at the airport. In a half hour I would leave, unless I stayed. I wanted to stay. I wished that he would ask me to stay, that in just one moment of weakness he would ask me not to go. But I knew that he would not. His asking me to give up my dream would be unconscionable. I knew that I could not stay either. I never felt that staying was God's will.

The silence between us deepened. The minutes were running too fast. He took my hand and placed it over his heart.

"This week has been the best week of my life. I am so blessed." His voice was wistful.

I was fighting back the tears, but close to losing the fight. "I don't want to go. Please don't let me go!"

"Let God finish the work that He has started in you."

"My heart is breaking."

"There is a bigger purpose in all this."

"It hurts."

"You must go."

"But my heart is breaking."

"I'll be praying for you."

AJ tried, but I was uncomforted. Like comforting a child who is afraid, he held me; like a father reassuring a heartbroken daughter, he held me; like a love unwilling to let go, he held me.

"It's time to go. You must."

Chapter 10

No One Is Born with Knowledge

Quietly, and quickly, I fell back into the routine of medical school. On the surface I was the same freshman with a ready smile and friendly attitude. However, my recent experiences had redefined and changed my outlook in many unseen ways. I was haunted by a new knowledge that the smile from a loved one today could be the last, and that a call from home may not always mean good news. Here, some of my innocence was forever gone, replaced by a sense of deep unrest. Emotions such as sadness, melancholy, fear, doubt, and stress that were so recently unknown to me were, now, my constant companions. But I had to keep going. There was no space to fully feel or entertain these new and disturbing emotions.

"God, will you be my study partner? Will you hold my hand?" I prayed as I re-focused all I had on my studies. But there were days when it would have been so much easier to walk away and go home. Things did not get easier with the passage of time. There was no truth in that saying, at least not for the study of medicine. Only the challenges and degree of difficulties change, and as soon as one task was mastered, another would surface. That said, some classes for me, like Biology, mirrored a walk in the park while others were like running an uphill marathon with no way of passing the baton to another. We were expected to keep running, carrying the baton to the assigned end. For me those uphill battles were Anatomy and Cadaver Dissection.

My comprehension of the Spanish language was slowly getting better, and I accepted as natural the giggles and raised eyebrows at my accent. Despite my steady progress and past successes, I was intensely plagued by fear of outright failing, not just a class but medical school itself. This was not an unfounded fear. Four members from our study group of nine had already given up. The constant pressure of studying or having a failing grade in too many classes to catch up were some of the reasons cited.

From a starting class of 115, we were already close to under one hundred. It was also rumored that more of us would drop out, as time progressed, the demand and degree of difficulty increased, and burn out set in.

I shared my concerns with Ma-ma; she reassured me that I would make it. She supported her reassurance with strong words of encouragement, reminding me of her constant intercessory prayers on my behalf. She also repeated many of our favorite Bible verses of God's sustaining grace.

But just when I thought I had managed to calm my fears, Otti burst in the room and announced that Veronica called it quits. "A Master's in Public Health seems more attractive," Otti continued. "She was tired of the constant stress of testing and deadlines to meet."

I was upset by the unexpected news. Veronica was one of my roommates. I couldn't quickly shrug off this news since she was considered a good student, doing better than others. Veronica's decision caused me to start doubting even more my own long-term survival. It was in such a state of mind that I found myself rushing to my final class for the day, Pharmacology.

""DC! Wait up!" Martin called. I slowed my pace and he easily caught up. "I have not seen much of you of late," he said.

"Busy studying, trying not to fail."

"You won't fail," he said with confidence. I eyed him, suspiciously wondering what he knew that I did not.

"I know that fear," he continued. "It has robbed me of many a night's rest."

He is only saying that to be nice, I thought. We all know that he is a walking library.

"Don't look so surprised!" he continued. "At every stage I have had that one class that had me worried, scared if you asked me… you will have those, too."

"Which was your most challenging?" I asked.

"Not which was, rather which is. Don't forget I'm still in school, too. At present it's Endocrinology, the hormones and its pathways. I'm finding it quite burdensome."

Martin suddenly sounded tired. For the first time I noticed the bags under his eyes. The few strands of premature grays were more pronounced. His tall frame looked a bit hunched over today.

A brief silence followed; it was not as if I've never heard it said before, but this time it made an impact. "DC, it's one word at a time. One page at a time. One class at a time. Consistency and hard work win the day. No one was born with this knowledge. Even the presumed brightest minds have to study. Truth be told, the so-called brightest among us may have just studied the hardest."

It was not lost on me where he placed his emphasis, one page, one class, and even more emphasis on consistency and hard work.

"Here is a clue for you," he continued. "You must identify your strengths in every subject matter, in every class and maximize them. Master them 100%. Afterwards, for the so-called weak, problem areas, work incredibly hard to compensate. You must always fill in all the gaps in your knowledge base. When you find gaps, don't accept them. For example, I always find the anatomy material to be easy for me, so I look for the anatomical points in Endocrinology. I study and learn them to the point where I will score 100% on every anatomy-like question. Then to compensate for the endocrine hormones, my so-called weak areas, I buckle down and worked even harder."

"How did that technique measure out for you in terms of final grades?" I asked.

"I never reveal my scores. Never," he said, with a laugh. "But there are times when accepting a pass was all I could do at the time."

Martin's voice was that of a seasoned final year medical student, soon to be a graduate who would face internship and residency. As he spoke, I gained a new understanding of how best to study and grasp such immensely complex information that I must not only read, but learn, understand, and remember to be a competent physician. No longer would I ignore my weak areas. No longer would I accept the gaps in my knowledge. I would face them with equal importance, and work at them until dominance was achieved. That was my easy promise at the moment. But fear and doubt does not give up without a fight and I found myself asking, "What if I am weak in everything in all classes?"

"Our Creator is just, no one is weak at everything. Otherwise we would give up too easily, maybe on life itself," he grumbled. "The flip side is that no one is good at everything, or else we would become unbearable — proud to the point of being foolish."

I could see why so many admired Martin, a refugee from wartorn Sudan. He lost more than half his family to war, lived in abject poverty, faced insurmountable hardship, and yet here he was not only writing his own survival story, but pulling others to get closer to theirs.

"Find your strength. Take courage. We were all given a measure of courage. Face your weak areas. A measure of fear will always be there. We all have fear. Fill in the places where you are lacking. Be deliberate. Work and then work some more. And while you are at it, pray. Then you will succeed."

"I will."

"Will you, Diane?" It was more like a challenge, less like a question. "You know you can, right? I mean, look how far you have come. One year gone and counting."

"I will succeed."

"I know you will."

"Thank you, Martin," The simple "thank you" did nothing to capture my heartfelt gratitude. "You know, I passed Anatomy!"

"Indeed, you did!" he said grinning.

"That success has a lot to do with your notes."

"But you worked for it. You and no one else studied those notes."

"Thank you either way." He nodded his head, accepting my "thank you."

"I have to go," I said quickly. "Dr. Joel does not take kindly to students arriving late for his lecture."

"I know. I had Dr. Joel for Pharmacology as well." I quickly ducked into the classroom seconds before Dr. Joel closed the door. He eyed me warily.

"The final awaits you," he said pointedly. His reminder of the dreaded finals did not evoke the fear and dread intended. A few minutes prior, it would have wrecked my peace of mind, but not now, not today, not ever thanks to my conversation with Martin. I was recharged, ready to push on. I was in a renewed state of mind, one word at a time, one page, one chapter, one book, one test, one year at a time. Failure was a myth.

With friends and family watching, I took the less-than-30-second walk to the platform and accepted my medical doctor diploma. The applause quickly died down as I slipped back into my seat. It was hard to believe: five years culminated in a one-minute walk. AJ and Ma-ma were not in attendance. Neither could be there even though they desired to be. Their absence was saddening. I knew, however, though absent, they were cheering me on. When I took that quick walk and the diploma was in my hands, I imagined them smiling at me.

On occasions like these, the emotions are usually high and varied: joy mixed in with bone-felt fatigue, tears, disbelief. It's over! I, Diane Carol, the country bumpkin, had made it through med school graduating in the top five of the class! Not first or second but, still, there among the first five of the over 90 graduates. I felt so many emotions that I decided to shelf, at least at that time.

I handed the diploma to my mother. Her joy in that moment superseded mine. I was too tired to truly appreciate or entertain any emotion except the desire to sleep. With much effort I harnessed my attention back to the graduation speaker, Dr. Wilson. And though I fixed my eyes in her direction, my thoughts were elsewhere. All my missing was for home. If only I could be transported home in a second. Just when I thought the disappointingly boring, unmotivating, lackluster graduation speech would never end, it did. I may have been the first on my feet, weaving my way in and out of the crowd.

I exited the auditorium in great haste and in search of friends, especially Otti and Martin. For five years, Otti had been my sister and friend; it didn't matter our cultural differences, her native language Finnish, mine English. God painted her milk white with blond hair to the eyelashes, while He gave me the deepest brown eyes, chocolate skin, and the curliest of hair. But that was where our differences stopped. We bonded easily from the very first day we met. We talked together as sisters reunited after a long separation. As freshmen, we had decided we were going to walk the journey of our medical training together, and we did.

Somewhere in the mix God sent Martin, our senior, to join forces with us two floundering freshmen. He became more than a friend; he was our brother and mentor. Speed and accuracy — no one is born with knowledge — study hard — do it again

— persistence — get to it — were his rallying cries to get us going when we were floundering.

"God has given me all that I need to succeed," I told him once in defiance and desperation. When I was discouraged, he would always remind me of that sentence.

"We should engrave our initials on her," I said to Otti and Martin whom I found sitting at our favorite spot. The old bench in front of the library knows our history. It carries years of secrets for us and many others — secrets that we can be thankful will never be uttered. The bench has sworn her secrecy to her students and has pledged her silence for our friendship. She was rarely alone. We spent many hours studying, arguing, and, yes, daydreaming of this very moment.

"We should," Otti agreed. "We should engrave not only our initials, but our hearts. Where did the time go?" Her voice was filled with faint regret.

"The next chapter of our journey is before us. Internship and residency training."

"Promises to be more impactful than medical school itself," Martin chimed in, finally joining the conversation. He had already completed his first year of internship and had moved on to his second year as an internal medicine resident.

"Let's promise to stay in touch."

"Yes, let's promise to write," responded Otti.

"We have our memories, and they are good ones."

"Yes, we have our memories . . ." Otti sounded wistful.

We sat quietly; the minutes passed us by as the silence grew heavier. We three were too alike for moments like these, each experiencing in our own way the emotions of our soon departure. Yet we knew there would be no crying. No outburst of emotions. None of us would acknowledge, much less voice, the obvious: this may be the last time we'd ever see each other.

THE LETTER

Otti was going back home to Finland to do specialty training in preventative medicine. Martin would continue his residency in internal medicine at Pan Am University in Texas. Returning home to Sudan to serve his country was his ultimate dream. My course for the time being was set for Galveston, Texas, where I was accepted for an internship transitional year in family and pediatric medicine. Soon, too soon, it was time to part. A new phase of the journey had begun for us.

Back in my dorm room, I found mom furiously packing away my final items in boxes and suitcases strategically placed all over the small floor space. She caught sight of me, standing in the doorway watching.

"Come, sweetie. Lay down and get your rest."

"No, let me help," I responded halfheartedly. She refused.

"You look worn and are expected in Galveston in a few hours."

Flopping on my bed, I reached for my Bible, the feel of the leaves always so fragile. Yet, it carried priceless, eternal life sustaining words. I tried to read, but my eyes would not cooperate; they were heavy with exhaustion. I closed the Bible and repeated my now favorite memorized one-line prayer:

"God, I love You first. I love You best. Help me to trust You in all ..." I fell asleep, never finishing the prayer. Falling asleep while praying was becoming too common for me lately.

Chapter 11

You Don't Have What It Takes

"Everything is bigger in Texas," so the saying goes. That includes egos, and the idea behind the saying itself.

The day I showed up at the sprawling University of Texas Medical Branch, otherwise called UTMB, I instantly knew that I was out of my element. So was every other intern; some just knew how to better hide the feeling of being overwhelmed, maybe afraid, even.

The dread of not knowing what to do was oppressive, especially now that we were running around in long white coats, stethoscopes hanging around our necks, and were now called "doctors." Life and death decisions were now ours to make. An air of apprehension followed us, the new medical interns, but in spite of all the worries, we were thrilled to be part of something so grand and distinctively important. We were wide-eyed, filled with hope and expectation. After all, we were no longer medical students; we were now medical doctors undergoing our first year in our area of specialty.

It was this wide-eyed hope and expectation that caused me to hearken back to medical school to compare then and now. Comparing events, situations, people, and experience is such a human trait. Compared to my current reality, medical school seemed so much easier and kinder. But that was the past; now I had to leave it behind in order to come to terms with present reality. Part of this present reality was the existence of an intense overlapping policy of supervision that occurs during any level of a doctor in training, be it internship, residency, or fellowship. The medical student is watched by the intern; the intern is watched by the first-year resident; the first-year resident by the second-year, the second by the third and so on. The final layer of supervision of the doctor in training was done by the attending medical doctor. In layman's language the attending is the "real" doctor. Then again there was the Medical Director, the Chair of Medicine, the Dean and finally the Board of Medicine. Therein lies the ultimate responsibility for safeguarding the patient care and training content of every doctor in this complex overlapping system. Our unspoken, unwritten rule was no room for error: do no harm. Do no harm even when dealing with the unknown. No room for error even in the unexpected.

This system of checks and balances, loosely put, is in pursuit of clinical perfection … error free at all cost, learning and practicing while "doing no harm." Medical school was sleepless, always on the go, with time for nothing else. Internship was its master—a tediously demanding one at that. During my training, I came across two distinct styles of attendings (doctors who train others to become doctors): One style could be described as kind and effective while carrying the proverbial big stick. This style inspired confidence and the deep desire to do one's very best. The other style was more of the big stick. This style also inspired confidence and the deep desire to do one's very best--but we students usually need a bit more tums-more upset stomach was experienced.

Dr. Rice was head of neonatology. Her "fame" preceded her; she, indeed, cast a long shadow. Though I had long heard of her exploits, not until I was at the end of my 14 month internship/residency training at UTMB was I assigned to her team. Up until then I was doing well, and had a reasonably excellent track record. I was not in the least bit bothered by the stories that were whispered about her. I also had my faith in God. This faith led me to believe that I could do all things with God's help. Up to this point, this faith along with hard work and much prayer had proven unstoppable.

The time I spent under Dr. Rice, however, challenged that belief! To the intern, she seemed aloof and unruffled. Some deemed her tough, others maybe a bit uncaring--for me she was still unknown. She never smiled; she spoke in a low, even-toned, unhurried manner, with deliberate emphasis on every word. Her hair cut almost to the style of a mohawk and her tall imposing frame made her even more fearsome.

The Texan cowgirl is how I imagined her at times, dressed in a broad brim hat, wide-legged pants, well fitted at the waist with a gun holster on her hip, complete with the wicked, pointed cowgirl boots. Except that instead, she wore a white coat done up with a badge that stated, "Medical Doctor," and had a stethoscope hanging from her neck. Whenever she would arrive for teaching rounds, it was not quite clear if we, her students, should stand at attention or take cover under the patient's bed.

All was going as expected, and I was fairly content, until that cloudy white morning when I crossed paths with Dr. Rice. She was not only my supervisor but also my head-attending in the area of her specialty. I was a bit late for her rounding/lecture session and although she didn't utter a word of disapproval, that arched eyebrow she gave me was enough. From that day forward, whenever I rounded with Dr. Rice I always felt unprepared, ill at ease, and out of place. I felt ten years old again, walking barefooted alone to school while carrying in my hand a pair of hand-me-down shoes way too big for my feet — crying because I hated school and was forced to go anyway. The feeling I had then was the exact same feeling I have every time I rounded on patients with her.

By completing medical school, I assumed I had already proven I had a brain. I worked relentlessly to make sure my placement in medical school and my scores in my USMLE Step 1, 2 and 3 (US medical licensing exams), a non-negotiable requirement to initiate internship and residency in all training hospital programs in the U.S. and its territories, was very competitive, which in no small part qualified me to continue my training in the US.

It didn't matter if I knew every word on Dr. Rice's lecture sheet. The needle didn't move if I correctly diagnosed and treated every case given. It remained the same. From the beginning to the end of the session, I would be ill at ease (palms sweaty, almost sick). Around her I found myself more nervous than when I experienced my first day as an intern. I felt brainless. How this "ill ease" began was always in doubt; but, one thing was for sure: we were never on the same page.

The intern/resident disagreeing with the supervising attending was never a good thing. It could spell the end real fast, especially if word got around to the other supervising physicians. You became a bullseye target, relentlessly watched. It did not help that on more than one occasion, I arrived late to Dr. Rice's rounding sessions. Today was one such day. The last word was barely uttered from the neurologist's lips when I began my run-walk routine from one end of the immensely huge hospital to the next in order to get to Dr. Rice's rounds. It did not help that both sessions were back to back. I lingered at the door, bent over, trying to catch my breath from the marathon I just ran.

A dilemma was brewing. I dared not miss her round. It's just not allowed without prior approval as even with approval it was stigmatized. Another colleague would have to pick up the slack, and the patient still needed to be seen. There is nothing worse in medicine than patient abandonment. There were procedures I needed to learn that day, like how to safely suction fluids from a patient's lung. By now I was a good five minutes late. I decided to sneak in at the back and with luck, slip in undetected. She was in the middle of a demonstration of a procedure. Hovered around, in rapt attention, were the other interns/residents. All were saintly on time. I felt then that I didn't belong.

"Late again, Dr. DC," she voiced weirdly. Her eyes never left her object. Yet she knew it was me. I had hoped that she would continue with her teaching and ignore me, but not today. She began to pepper me with questions: "Describe the common complications of thoracentesis?"

Easy enough, I thought, as I answered. I stayed up practically all night reviewing the subject. But she was relentless. She would not be outdone. My being up studying all night was no match for her training and years of experience, and she knew it. My colleagues knew it and, most importantly, I knew it, too. She did not stop her questioning until I no longer knew the answer. Even if it was a question still under research she probably would have used it to prove her point. She was masterful.

"Late and unprepared for my lecture," she stated. I may have heard a tinge of vindication.

"I came the moment I was finished with..."

She held up her hand. "No excuse," she said. Every intern knows that silence is a winner when faced with a supervisor who showed the slightest hint of displeasure, but in my desperation to make it right, I continued.

"Only it's not an excuse. I could not abandon one patient for another, per guidelines."

"You hope to point me on guidelines?"

"Yes, I mean, no, of course not," I mumbled, hearing the warning bells that went ignored. I was about to mutter another defensive line when I was discreetly, but forcefully, elbowed into silence by another intern.

Every person has a moment when they wish they had not opened their mouths only a second after they did, the moment you wish you could disappear and start over, the moment you wish you could turn back the clock to a time more favorable. Today was my moment.

Dr. Rice directed her attention back to her procedure, but not before requesting to speak with me in her office at the conclusion of the session. We all knew then that the possibility of my being kicked off her team, or worse, was highly likely. She would have the support of the handbook, the one that I was made to sign after I had been given a copy and understood its contents. Repetitive tardiness was right up there as a reason for disciplinary action.

When I woke up that morning, if you had asked me to write the ticket to my day, sitting in Dr. Rice's office was a scenario that would never in a million years have crossed my mind. Having been sent to the principal's office was exactly what it felt like. It was unnerving, a first in my educational journey. I had no reference point of what to truly expect.

I was hopeful that she would not take me off her team. "The unpardonable — a persistently raised red flag — the at-risk intern/resident-listed for closer scrutiny-on perpetual probation." These were some of the phrases my seniors used to describe the results of being in the cross hairs or booted off an attending doctor's team. Prayers of desperation leaped from my mind.

"Oh, God help me, please help me!" Oh, how I wish I had kept my mouth shut. I wish that I was not plagued with the habitual habit of tardiness to her hospital rounds. I wish that I knew all of the answers to her questions. I wish I did not cry when assigned by her to tell a mom their child will die or has died. "It was unbecoming of a doctor." Though it was not said, that was how I felt, especially as I heard of no one else who did in public. I wish that I was sophisticated and self-assured like my colleagues, that I didn't sound so foreign. I was yet to learn the show-off, impress-you game to my supervisor. They played to my weakness to highlight their presumed strength. When the truth is, some secretly asked for my help in order to impress Dr. Rice during her rounds.

I wish, I wish and I wish again . . .. but alas.

As I waited nervously, I got tired of the wishing game and took the time to look around. Dr. Rice's awards were many: Resident of the Year, Chief Resident, Outstanding Fellow, on and on. Inquisitiveness had overtaken me; I was still peering at them when she walked in and sat down in her comfortable oversized chair; she seemed in no hurry to tell me my fate. It was hard to read her expression, but harder was the wait. Maybe she forgot why I was summoned. Maybe if I snuck out, she wouldn't notice.

Then she spoke with that distinctive Texan accent, "Dr. DC, you're at the middle of your four-week rotation and you're still not meeting my expectations. Your unpreparedness for my lectures is concerning and your habitual tardiness is a violation of the university handbook guidelines."

If she heard my apology for my tardiness, and if my promise to never let it happen again moved her, she was not about to show me. The flicker of hope that I was looking for was not there. She remained unnaturally quiet after my apologies. I thought that I was convincing. She dismissed my rebuttal and continued as if I had not spoken.

"Your participation in my rotation has been unsatisfactory." This was followed by a long pause, after which she rendered what seemed to be her final evaluation. "Dr. DC, I don't believe you have what it takes to become a doctor." She spoke with authority and confidence.

"I have been successful in all my other rotations," I countered.

Her eyes warned me to speak no further. For a brief second, I almost believed her. *I don't have what it takes?*

"God has given every man everything he needs to succeed, including the right to fight for himself and the know-how to defend his possession," Ma-ma would say by way of telling me that it was okay to speak up for myself. Except I am sure when Ma-ma made her uttering she would have never conjured up the likes of Dr. Rice. She was probably thinking more of our equals — the poor, humble, rural, barely educated folks. But as I sat there I knew Ma-ma would have fully expected me to assess the situation and not to follow suit and count myself out. She would have expected me to fight for myself and succeed.

THE LETTER

I did assess my situation: I had already successfully completed five grueling years of medical school while learning a second language. I was now fluent in Spanish. Since my arrival at UTMB, I had completed almost 24 months of clinical rotations with many excellent evaluations from other attendings, who were her peers. All of my exams scores were very competitive, but two weeks into a four-week rotation, she wrote me off as if a bad debt. "Ya right," I felt like saying and more, but she was my attending. I was the student, and maybe of all the attendings she was the only one who was right. I just didn't have what it takes.

Oddly, for the first time since we crossed paths, I was no longer fearful. My heart was no longer beating wildly. My palms were still sweating, but it didn't matter. I had them securely hidden in my lap, where she could not see them in case they began shaking. I knew that I was training to become an MD, not because I had things handed to me, but because God was at work helping me along the journey. That belief kept me going even when I didn't believe much in my chances. Maybe I was naive.

If she only knew that my sitting across from her immensely beautiful table and walking the halls of this prestigious hospital was proof of what God can do for anyone who asked Him. Because I knew this, it was impossible for me to accept her assertion. Yet she was influential and she knew it.

She stood up, sending me back to my daily duties, an indication that she was through with me, at least for now. I had a feeling that this would not be the last of it. I was about to make a hasty exit when I found myself asking her if a camel could fit through a keyhole. The mask, the one of calm indifference she had throughout the meeting, crumbled. It was replaced with one of shock at my audacity of asking her such a profoundly foolish question.

Yet I repeated the question, just to make sure she heard it. "Can a camel be fitted through a keyhole?"

Without a second thought she replied. "No one can fit a camel through a keyhole." She kept her tone dead even; it hid her irritation. *Outside of medicine, I will believe nothing she tells me*, I decided as I walked back to my post.

How could she not believe in the "camel-through-keyhole" moments? There were just too many in history for me not to believe. My math tutor had already browbeaten me with stories of Thomas Edison and the light bulb to get me to keep trying. Marie Curie, who developed radium, was her all-time favorite. "The way of progress was neither swift nor easy," was one of her favorite quotes from Curie. I knew I was no Edison, further yet from being a trail-blazer like Curie, but a little bit of perseverance never hurt. I debated in my head. The voices of my Ma-ma's education were already pounding in my head as I planned ahead. I also knew I had it within me to out-work, out-study, out-perform every single challenger. I just had to be up to the task.

But every effort of self-encouragement could not stop me from worrying. I knew things would never be the same. I was on this woman's radar and it was not in a good way. There was for me now a different standard — absolutely no room for error. No tolerance for not knowing. Yet I was only a lonely intern/resident. I was still in training, still needing her supervision, instruction, and guidance. I needed to find a way to get back in her favor.

Days later I was still reeling from my meeting with Dr. Rice. I was one year plus into my training, and I was moving along successfully, and just like the other interns and residents, I was meeting expectations, rotation after rotation. But she spoke and everything changed. I was now feeling like a non-swimmer on a ledge about to fall off into the deep sea. I was surprised at how much her words affected me. There were days when part of me doubted and questioned the very worthiness of my presence at UTMB. Such a noble institution should be beyond my reach. Making it worse, going forward Dr. Rice would call ahead at each of my scheduled rotations, informing her colleagues of her position regarding my future as a medical doctor. I knew only because one of my attending physicians remarked she was happy my work was not as she was told, and gave me all above average markings.

Dr. Rice, however, was singular in her purpose. I was scrutinized more closely if that was even possible. My clinical documentation was searched for errors. My presentations were examined with eagle eyes. It was a time of unbelievable pressure. During rounds, I was afraid of giving the incorrect answer. I was reluctant to ask questions. A trainee not asking questions? Unthinkable. Should I be silent? Should I ask my questions and confirm the now preconceived notion that I would not make it, that being a doctor was just not for me? The whispers got louder. As expected, news spread and grew in numbers. The situation was almost unbearable.

It was hard at times to show up on Dr. Rice's rounds, making it even more difficult to keep up the day-to-day momentum. I understood why some of my colleagues chose to avoid me; after all, who would not avoid a sinking ship? It was tough and lonely. But every day I woke up and put one foot in front of the other. I was forcing myself not to think of tomorrow. I was focusing only on winning today's battle. Each day I'd arrive early, and stay long after my duty was over. I could be found in the hospital among the patients, searching their charts. I was looking for a way to put the camel through the keyhole. I would maximize my strong points, consistently working very hard on my weak areas, always filling in the gaps.

"On your peace hangs this test," my upper level resident whispered as we walked towards the great hall. In that hall every intern and resident of every specialty of medicine known to man will find their names, take their seats, and begin taking the In-training exam. Whether it was in cardiology, dermatology, neurosurgery or any of the many other areas of medicine, there was no going forward without this yearly test taking. The attending responsible for training us paid very close attention to the score we received. You will be either cheered and rewarded or cornered for more studying.

"Imagine seven continuous hours of taking an exam. A marathon, who can survive that?" one of us said.

"Us. We are expected to. We have to. It's made to test not only our knowledge base, but also our ability to concentrate and make right decisions when tired," another moaned.

"Not to mention our endurance and our ability to stay sane under stress," came back the other. "And the hardest, longest questions and weirdest case scenario with a matching picture are saved up for the last hour."

"Deliberately so because its when we are at our weakest physical and mental state, we are likely to make mistakes."

"Highest risk of causing harm," another sighed.

"Thank you for telling me more than I needed to hear." It was my turn to sigh.

"Yep," she retorted.

"And for reminding me of the ant nest we are about to face."

I didn't need this conversation with Dr. Leng to feel nervous. I had already taken the allowed daily dose of tums to calm the burn in my nervous gut. There was no practice test to take in preparation for this exam. It was a test to reveal the raw knowledge base left over from medical school, in addition to clinical medical information currently learned.

The day prior, Dr. Rice reminded us of the upcoming exam. She was less than subtle in stating her prognostication. She knew those who would do well. I was not one of them.

Oddly, her prognostication did not dissuade me. I assume it was because she was feeling nervous for us, and by extension, herself. After all, we were a reflection of her; our failures and successes invariably pointed back to our training.

And so, the test began, but not before I prayed a short prayer asking for God's divine help. During the last hour of the seven-hour test, everything hurt. I was sure that I was beginning to have double vision. It didn't help that more than half of the test takers had already turned in their test papers, an indication that they were through. Or were they giving up in sheer exhaustion?

I was among the last to leave the great hall, after having to hurry through the final questions seconds before the last minute. I exited the examination hall and there they were with long faces. It was beyond my understanding why after every test, we test takers would hang around and torture ourselves further by discussing the likely questions that we missed. Worse yet, we dared to compare the different responses. But we did just that, making ourselves more miserable, and vulnerable, in the process.

"I guess we'll know for sure in two weeks," someone griped before wandering off.

Two weeks later, I stood before Dr. Rice's office waiting to be invited in. I was not summoned; the meeting was by my own request. I wanted to discuss my exam results. I not only scored the highest test score among my peers, but outperformed the national average. The Program Director awarded me a letter of congratulations for the record, and a twenty-dollar Starbucks gift card. Despite all that, deep down it was Dr. Rice's approval that mattered. Her congratulating me would be major; it would land me on the moon.

"I guess no one can complain about that," was her short response to the news before turning back to whatever important matter she had at hand. I had hoped that my test score results would have lessened her expressed concern that my knowledge base was on shaky ground. She seemed unimpressed. I thanked God, anyway, for His help and still managed a self-satisfied smile. It felt good to prove her wrong. *God, You're awesomeness!*

In time, my rotation with Dr. Rice drew to a close. Though this rotation was the same length of time as all the others, it felt like my longest rotation ever! That rotation firmly behind me, several pounds lighter, with less than discreet bags under my eyes and bone weary,

I moved on to the next assigned rotations. It was the area of infectious diseases.

"This body of study will serve you well, whether you follow through to missionary work overseas or stay local," Dr. Karen, the Infectious Diseases Specialist in charge, said reassuringly.

I nodded in anticipation.

"You will learn about all sorts of interesting infections and how to identify, prevent and treat them."

She was still in mid-sentence when a patient's chart was placed in my hand.

"She is one month old with fever and irritability."

"Possible meningitis?" I queried. Fresh off my month's rotation with Dr. Rice, I had seen samples of its presentation in the young infant. "Because they cannot complain of headache, they express irritability instead," I continued.

"Very good," my supervising resident said, sounding pleased.

"Will need a lumbar puncture to confirm."

"You're on it," she added with a grin. "So, you won't mind informing the mom of the plan of care?" Her tone sounded more like an order.

But I did mind. The idea of pushing a needle in a four-week-old child's back to suck out spinal fluid was daunting to me. Imagine making that request of the mom. Anger and a firm "No!" was not an uncommon response. The younger and more amateur the physician-in-training, the more confident the no-response. It was not unusual for the attending doctor to have to step forward and present the requests to the patient's family.

"Will you come while I get permission? This is my first time."

"No, you go alone, and don't come back if it's a no. I will be there to hold your hand for the procedure."

I took a deep breath before knocking and entering the patient's room. The infant not only looked ill and frail, but seemed smaller than her stated age of 4 weeks. The mother smiled shyly; her eyes looked at me determinedly unafraid, but worried. She was alone; I wished that she were not but that a husband, or grandma, just another person was sitting with her. I introduced myself and asked if I could hold the baby. I was there as her doctor, but I chose to engage her as a friend who was visiting and meeting the newborn for the first time. The infant wriggled in my arms, her hot skin against my cool hand was evidence of her persistent fever. Because there was no easy way to say it, I decided to just go ahead.

"Mrs. Sandie, your baby needs to be tested for meningitis, an infection affecting the brain. I will need to place a needle right here, to obtain some fluids from her brain for testing." I pointed towards the baby's lower back. "We need to do it right away in order to get her well so you can take her home."

Mrs. Sandie was silent for so long I thought that she may not have heard me. Finally, she nodded yes; I could tell that she was fighting to remain brave.

I entered the procedure room with the baby. The supervising resident was present to "hold my hand" as she had promised.

She was a good teacher, and she felt I was a good student, which was reflected by her response. "This was the best performed lumbar puncture yet. Well done." The attending doctor later nodded toward me on her way out, as news of my lumbar puncture "expertise" reached her.

A smile formed on my lips as I walked. A good first day in a new rotation is always the best way to start.

"Let's go celebrate with some free food," my supervising resident suggested, pointing toward the hospital cafeteria.

I reluctantly declined, not because I was not hungry. Catching up on some much-needed sleep was the only thing on my mind. If I stopped to eat I would delay the process by another hour. I was already so sleep deprived I was running on fumes.

"See you tomorrow, and early?" She waved me off smiling.

"Bright and very early," I responded, smiling back. It felt nice. I was feeling a sense of happiness. I had forgotten how good that felt.

In what seemed like the blink of an eye, I made it through the infectious disease rotations. I relished the positive feedback. I had a good month. In the process I developed a deep interest and love for the specialty area of infectious diseases and began to contemplate the likelihood of specializing in that area myself. I was, however, happy to keep moving.

One more rotation to cross off the list. Next in line was my rotation in the adrenaline-filled intensive care unit, followed by hormone-driven endocrinology. Then it was the cardiology, followed By intestine-moving gastroenterology, which was to be my final rotation to end the academic year. I was overcome with great relief and I was happy. Another year was behind me. I was one step closer to finishing. But I was apprehensive. It meant the end-of-year evaluation, and Dr. Rice was waiting.

I fidgeted nervously with my pen and though I was waiting but a few minutes it seemed like eternity. I was moments away from learning whether or not I had been offered the customary promotion on to the next year of my residence training.

On the very first day of our training, the large gathering of interns was informed by the Program Director that we did not have a contractual agreement to begin or complete the process. There was no expressed or implied guarantee of promotion to each year's training. It was, rather, a year-by-year "promotion by invitation based on merit." The longer I waited the more anxious I became. I wavered between faith and doubt. Faith, because I have always believed that God can do anything, for anyone. Faith, because so many prayers had gone up to the God of heaven on my behalf.

"You are His child; He caused you to be; you can trust Him to help you." Ma-ma would repeat the phrase time and again to encourage me along, a phrase I have come to believe wholeheartedly since childhood.

Still, pangs of anxiety and doubt crept in. What if I were not promoted to continue my training? What would I do next? Where would I go? Without completing my residency and my specialty training, my five years of medical school would be all for nothing. Without it I could not practice medicine. Would my dream of becoming a doctor be suddenly over? My faith seemed helpless in the face of such pelting questions. "You do not have what it takes to become a doctor." Dr. Rice's words would randomly pop into my subconscious thoughts, and even though I never truly believed her declaration, there were times I wondered if she were right. Because the mind tends to more readily believe the negative over the positive, the pain over the pleasure, chaos over order, I found my mind dwelling more on Dr. Rice's words than the other attendings who believed and stated the contrary. Dr. William, Head of the Department of Nephrology, my attending supervisor, disagreed and took her view all the way to the Chair of Medicine. "DC is right there with the best of the lot," was her argument. "She should be given the same chances," was what she later told me by way of encouragement.

But every day that I was Dr. Rice's resident, her smileless, disapproving countenance sought to reinforce her sentiment. Oddly, there was not a time when I remembered feeling like packing it in and walking away — not once. I continued to wait.

While waiting, I tried hard not to surrender to fear. There was also an ongoing battle in the back of my subconsciousness between fear and doubt and the soft voice of Scriptures, memorized since my childhood.

In broken bits they came—God hath not given us a spirit of fear but of power and of love and of a sound mind—I can do all things through Him ... 2 Timothy 1:7 KJV, Philippians 4:13 KJV.

Chapter 12

Not So Sure Anymore

"Let me start by saying that you could not have gotten this far without smarts, hard work, and determination." No niceties, no small talks. A quick handshake and the meeting commenced. All the while, Dr. Grant, the Medical Director, spoke as he simultaneously leafed through my file. I watched him as he looked up past me while I tried unsuccessfully to make eye contact. The human eye always tells the story better than the lips. I wanted his eyes to tell me the final decision. He would not make eye contact.

"I have here several letters from families of patients you have cared for."

Complaints? All doctors in training know that there exists no greater source of irritation for the supervising attending, than complaints from patients or family against the residents whom they are training. It's seen as a reflection of their ability to train well.

"Mrs. Sandi," he continued, "sent a letter regarding a lumbar puncture that you performed on her child. She wants to commend the hospital for training compassionate future doctors. Your name is mentioned."

He looked pleased. A nod to a resident in his training was a nod to him.

"Here, for your wall." He handed me a plaque, and a thank you card from another family whom I had helped in their decision to get hospice care. It was a Spanish-speaking family. The plaque bore evidence that English was a second language they were still learning. But the error in language made the sentiments more beautiful to me.

Dr. Grant was deliberate in going through each piece of paper placed in my file. At some point I had stopped listening, waiting rather for just one phrase: "Welcome back," or "Congratulations!" But that was not what I heard.

"What do you mean I am not a good fit for your program? What about all the other attending evaluations? Why not validate their assessment? What do you think as program director? You said it was only hard work and smarts that took me this far. Tell me the objective reasons so I can work on them?" These are a few of the many unspoken questions that passed through my mind as Dr. Grant spoke, but I was no longer listening to my soon to be ex-program director. The dream that I worked for so tirelessly for so many years was no more. As if housed in a fragile jar which was flung against a giant wall of steel and shattered, it lay splattered at my feet in irretrievable dust.

There were no tears or self-pity, just a sense of being beaten. I was past feeling tired, overcome by a weariness that was felt to the bone. A month of continuous sleep would not suffice.

Resting my head on the uncomfortable oversized seat, I closed my eyes, willing myself to sleep but without success. It was the countdown to my final hours of a rather interesting three-day journey on the famed Greyhound Bus from Texas to New York City. Traveling by way of the Greyhound Bus, I entered a new world with its fascinating sights and sounds. Since leaving home for medical school, my orbit was exclusive only to the hospital among doctors, along with the sick and dying. That was my life and all I knew of the USA. Here on the Greyhound, a different world continued to unfold before me. At one of the three bus changes into my travel, I came face to face with the homeless wanderer. He told me he was going from city to city in search of a wonderful life. He knew there was something grand out there that he wanted to obtain, except when asked he could not put a name to it. The doctor in me was making a guess of an undiagnosed mental illness. His flight of ideas was beyond fantasy and hard to follow.

I also met a middle-aged musician who left home upon the first hour of turning eighteen; he too was en-route to his big break in the music world. Then there were the permanent dwellers at the bus station, hustling out a livelihood, selling small items. And like any other mode of travel there was the young mother traveling with two young kids. The youngest was not impressed with the journey, fussy and crying for the better part of the long bus ride. The Greyhound journey, without doubt, possessed a culture of its own. As I observed the line of newcomers waiting to board the bus, I wondered which character would join the seat that had just become available beside me.

The bus rumbled along, sometimes bumpy, other times smoothly; it reflected my thoughts. My three-day bus ride was close to its end, yet I was still undecided. I debated between spending my "off time" in New York with my uncle Henry, or catching the first available flight from John F. Kennedy Airport, homeward bound.

I craved the silence and lack of prodding that the time with my uncle in New York would offer me. I was still rattled from recent events and had no wish to revisit them. If I were not to continue my medical training, I needed peace and quiet in order to re-evaluate my next step — to decide what to do with my life. The elephant in the room was how to tell those I loved that I had failed? I hoped no one would say, "I told you so." I hoped I would not be spurned for making a go at something different and failing. "It may be best to stay with my uncle," I reasoned. He was a man of few words, and asked fewer questions.

THE LETTER

"You ok, Lady Di?" was the most I would sometimes get from him a few times a day. I loved my uncle; his ability to help without questioning was uniquely remarkable as a member of a talkative family.

On the other hand, going home meant sharing every minute detail of events of my life while away in training. Ma-ma would leave no stone unturned. Her voice was already in my subconscious, advising me on my next move while admonishing me to trust God in spite of my woes and setbacks. I was not ready to hear it, let alone follow it. I felt let down. God did not answer my prayers. I intended to have my pity party, a party Ma-ma would not attend; in fact, she would probably crash it.

"This is my stop." The voice of the traveler occupying the seat beside me lured me back to the moment. "Goodbye, and thank you for the book," she said, smiling and hugging it to her chest.

The book, The Wounded Healer by Henri Nouwen, was intended to be my three-day traveling companion, but it was not to be. She had hopped on the Greyhound Bus on its stop in Louisiana, sharing the seat with me all the way to Florida. As she freely shared the story of her childhood I listened, at first resisting the intrusion to the silence and peace I craved, but her persistence wore me down. I relented and gave her my undivided attention; there was no end to her sad stories. As I listened, I heard with understanding. I too was feeling unsure of my next step. The path that once looked so clear seemed a thing of the past. Like her, I too was feeling letdown. My once ambitious dream and assured faith in God's leading had taken wings and flew away without giving me time to say goodbye. It was all so sudden. In its place lay bewilderment and uncertainty of the future.

It was my turn to disembark. The sights and sounds of New York City were all it was said to be and more. Even my current reality could not suppress the wonder and excitement that being in New York evoked. The hustle was palpable. The pace was frightful.

The sea of human faces was remarkable. New York spoke survival, a place not for the faint of heart.

Pulling my heavy book-laden suitcase, I approached the line of the famed New York yellow cab waiting ahead. "JFK airport, please," I said. My yearning for home had won. I chose home.

I sat for hours, intently scrolling through ERAS, the Electronic Residency Application Service website. At Ma-ma's insistence I decided to re-apply to continue my medical training. Finding another residency program willing to allow me the chance to resume my specialty training was more daunting than I had feared. It was no longer a matter of being accepted on the strength of finishing medical school and passing the USMLE-United States Medical Licensing. That criteria no longer applied to me. I now had to explain my worthiness. My medical training had been interrupted. Dr. Rice had given her verdict, and for many training programs her word was law. In addition, I needed three letters of recommendation from my prior training hospital. Dr. Rice, head of her department, and Dr. Grant, the Program Director, each by default had to write one or at minimum give verbal input to whichever training program I applied to for entry.

I wanted to lay low and tend to my wounds; however, Ma-ma kept telling me failure was a myth. God had a plan for my life, and that I was not to give up. She insisted that everything that was happening was God's way of making me a better person. Sometimes I felt Ma-ma lived in an alternate reality. Nothing seemed to phase her. The house could be ablaze and she would remain seated, believing the fire would leave her be.

Silence and a stony face was Ma-ma's dominant response as I continued to share what had happened.

"What if Dr. Rice is right?" I repeated.

"Except you know she was not," she calmly declared.

"And God, does He really care what happened to me?" I said rather carefully. I did not want to upset Ma-ma. She is not one to entertain my questioning God's dealings, as she put it.

"He has a plan for your life," her staple response.

"My prayers remain unanswered. I thought my outcome would have been different," I pleaded, wanting her to agree with me.

"Trust God's permissive will."

"A will that had me walk the halls with the whispers talking about my soon departure, their expression of pity, even —that was hard on me!" I was feeling a bit desperate. Short of stamping my feet and screaming, I tried as hard as I could to get her to come in line with how I was feeling. My emotions seemed inconsequential to her. Her silence was like a rebuke, a response in itself. "Ma-ma those who take no thought of God, shun the Bible, did quite fine, all invited back to continue their training. Why not me?"

Again, silence was all I got from Ma-ma. It did not dissuade me as I was determined to provoke the response I wanted. I wanted her to tell me that what happened to me was unfair, that my anger was justified, I was right in wanting to give up. I did not deserve this.

"And all this time I was doing exactly as you said. Pray, and do my work, and pray some more and work some more," I continued.

Silence.

"All your stories about hard work and faith, my useless test scores were above the national average. It was all for naught," I grumbled.

Silence.

"Ma-ma, are you listening?"

"I am."

"Then say something."

"What do you want me to say that I have not for the years I raised you? I have asked you to trust and rest in God."

"There it is, 'trust and rest.' I should have known. How about it's not fair!"

"Is a medical degree of greater importance than a godly character?" she asked pointedly.

"You ask that?"

"What do you want most? A God-given life of purpose, or what you think you are owed in this life?"

"Ma-ma! You know that I ..."

" ... Do you think because you're a follower of Christ and His teachings that you'll have no cross to bear in this world? No disappointments, no broken dreams as you see them? If that's what you have learned from me, then I have misrepresented the teachings of the Bible, and by extension, life itself."

"I worked, I fasted, I prayed, what more...?"

"—Choose faith and trust His will for your life and not what you understand that will to be."

Her voice was so kind, her look so caring that it mirrored the disappointment and hurt I was feeling.

"I don't have your faith."

"I know it's hard, maybe unfair, undeserving at best ... but you just wait. Do it without murmuring or unnecessary worrying, none of which will change your reality."

It was my turn to be silent. This was not the conversation I wanted, and as expected, she crashed my pity party.

She allowed me to feel the pain of my lost dream but refused to encourage or join in my self-pity. Hours later I was still where she left me, lying on the bare hardwood floor, a pillow over my face. I did not feel like praying; even when I tried, it felt hollow.

"God please don't abandon my dreams. Please help me! I somehow messed things up. What is to become of me? I have no influence, no ideas, no nothing."

Through this crucial time, Ma-ma refrained from giving me advice. It was as if she was done raising me, leaving me to chart my own path, with God as my guide. It was almost as if she was daring me to choose wallowing in self-pity or finding my way. It was up to me now. She was done holding my hand. But I knew that she was still praying for me. I often found her kneeling by her bedside, her face rested in her palm. The Bible was always opened beside her kneeling frame. At times, her prayers were loud as if wanting me to hear her requests on my behalf. Other times all I heard was her groaning. My name was not the only name that poured from her lips as she fervently prayed.

Days later, I got a call.

"Diane, this is Loida. I have not heard from you for a while."

The voice on the other end of the line brought me a smile. "I have gone underground," I half-joked.

Loida was a persistent friend. We met while I was in my first year of medical school; she was in nursing school. Our friendship continued long after we parted company. Despite her busy life as a top-notch RN in California, it seemed she kept her pulse on all events in her friends' lives. She was my go-to person if I needed to reconnect with a lost friend. She had the unique talent of having and maintaining a broad network of friends in all professional fields, from all walks of life, and hailing from many countries.

She developed this talent as a pastor's daughter. Her sermons were acts of kindness, making the connections, getting the answers others sought. She was best at being the one to always do the reaching out in our friendship, always present for the highs and the lows of my journey.

"What are you up to?" she asked.

"Filling out applications and re-applying to get back into residency training."

"That reminds me. They are looking for a second-year resident in Rome, Georgia. There is another opening in San Juan, Puerto Rico. Both vacancies are from military personnel who got moved around."

She had my attention. "Did you say vacancies?"

"Yep, your colleagues just got shipped around."

"I bet it's hard," I reflected, mirroring my recent upheaval. "It's said that is what these military folks signed up for."

"Yes, and what did you sign up for?"

"Did you speak to Ma-ma?" I asked, groaning inwardly.

"No, why?"

"Of late, Ma-ma's been asking me that question too many times in different ways, and now from you?"

"By the way, your spot from your prior hospital…"

"What about it?"

"It was filled by a returning military family. Young kids and a mother nearby. Her husband was deployed overseas."

My ears perked up. "How do you know all that?"

"I have my ears and eyes on the ground. You may be swapping places…who knows? You in Georgia or Puerto Rico, she in Texas."

"You think so?"

"God's ways are beyond ours. He checkmates all the time," Ma-ma whispered, eavesdropping on the conversation.

"True. By the way, I have a friend in Puerto Rico," Loida continued. "If you need help to get started I have her number."

"Only, I have never heard of Puerto Rico before."

"Language won't be a problem, now that you're bilingual," she said, laughing. "It's a bilingual US territory. There is a military base and a veteran hospital," she continued. It was almost as if she was nudging me forward.

"Listen, I have to go, but call the program in Puerto Rico or Georgia!" With that, she hung up.

"Apprehensive but happy," was the phrase I used as I described to my sister how I felt that I had gotten back into my medical training. "And this time in the state of Georgia," I said.

THE LETTER

"Please, be careful," she cautioned. "Don't act too smart, count your words, remember the saying, 'When in Rome do like the Romans do.' Please," she begged.

No one knew me better than my sister. Yes, she was the eldest, but it didn't stop me from bossing her around. She was worried that I might treat others the same in my new role. Although my sister was living alongside our mom in Germany, we remained very close and she was my truest confidant and advisor.

"I understand your good intentions," she continued. "I know that you want to share the good news of salvation as you call it, but stop preaching, and leave all your religious literature at home. You are there to become a doctor, not evangelize the place. Do what you need to do, finish and—get out!"

Her voice reflected her desperation. But even while my sister advised caution, I was already planning my next move. The debate on the Genesis creation in contrast to Darwin's evolution was for me an open season for sharing. Words like "evolution," or phrases like "poor protoplasm" were commonplace in the medical community. Yet the more I studied medicine the more I became convinced that what I've always believed was true: the human body was created; it did not evolve. The perfection of the cell just could not be random. But she made me promise not to get into anymore creation vs. evolution debates, nor invite any of my attendings to church, nor offer Bible studies to my colleagues.

"Please sis, don't do it," she cautioned before she hung up.

After several attempts, and getting lost too many times to count, the "Welcome to Georgia" sign came into sharp view.

Hours later, I found myself sitting across from the program director of internal medicine. His coordinator and chief resident were discussing what my schedule would be like. They welcomed me with open arms, acting as if they desperately needed a second-year resident. I came prepared to answer all questions, including the potentially hard ones related to my former program, but Dr. Lait seemed to have no interest in the past.

And so, again, I began the daily routine of a resident doctor's life. Four weeks later, I felt that I was a pro with the hospital charting and computer system. I knew my way around campus almost perfectly. As I walked briskly toward the hospital, I could not help but notice, as if for the first time, how the beautifully painted Georgian white blue sky hung precipitously against the midday sun. My pager suddenly interrupted my sense of peace, indicating that I was called to the medical director's office. It was not unusual to be called for impromptu meetings. I entered Dr. Lait's office, observing the coveted view that he had of the outside world. The carefully manicured lawn was the prettiest I had ever seen.

"I've just gotten your official letter from Dr. Rice, and she followed up with a call," Dr. Lait informed me. "Based on her recommendation, we will have to withdraw our offer."

I knew that I was dreaming. The good part to dreaming was that the moment I woke up it would be all gone. After all, I just purchased my first fixer upper house, and once and for all I rid myself of my old Ford, which more than once left me stranded on the highway. My signature on the dotted line for that car was, undoubtedly, still wet. Having just settled into the idea of going forward once and for all, my family gave me their full support in my new acquisition. Boy had I been praying, really hard.

Whatever it was that caused such an irk in Dr. Rice I did not want repeated. So, I knew that this was a dream, except it was not because the program director was pushing across the table a letter requesting me to sign. He wanted me to accept a three-month stipend in advance in exchange for not bringing a case against the program.

I didn't need his stipend, so I didn't sign. The only case that I intended to pursue with God was to the "Why?" Why was this happening to me? The case was how not to lose hope, how to fight the urge to believe that God left me, and how to respond to the thought that I made a huge mistake along the way and was just too blind to see. I would pray for an open door, everything would line up, and then the door would close. It was as if the battle for my future was between God and Dr. Rice, and she was winning. "Everything is going great" until she stands up and everyone else sits down. So it seemed. Presumed failure that happens repeatedly can begin to breed shame, self-doubt, discouragement and great fear.

The fear that one is flawed.

The fear that one is not good enough.

The fear that makes you want to give up.

That fear was beginning to bother me.

It seemed that my whole future hung on Dr. Rice's evaluation.

"Why, when there is more than a full year's worth of excellent evaluations for an intern from the other attending doctors?" my sister asked perplexedly over the phone.

And I could just hear Ma-ma's usual story: "God is working it out; He is refining you to be pure as gold. He has a plan for your life."

Part of me stopped believing and part of me believed. Part of me was becoming angry and part of me wondered if God cared not for my future. I could not shake off the feeling that maybe I made a mistake somewhere along the line.

While I sat across the desk looking at this stranger I met but four weeks ago, with whom I may never cross paths ever again, the strangest thing happened. The verse from 2 Timothy 1:7 came to mind: "God hath not given us the spirit of fear; but of power, and of love, and of a sound mind" (KJV)

I knew I was "brainwashed" by my grandma in the ways of the Bible, so when in that moment this particular Bible promise came to mind I felt it was likely autopilot. I could not have conjured up those words even with my best effort. Yet the idea of having love and a sound mind in this moment did not prevent me from the temptation of wishing to spout out some not too choice words to Dr. Lait, words that would rightly express my irritation at him for wasting four weeks of my time. I felt like asking him why he did not do his homework and gather all the information prior to accepting my application. I wanted to ask him if he did not have a mind of his own, if his own evaluation did not count for anything. Asking him those questions would have pleased me. After all, only the day before he said I was doing quite fine, fitting in splendidly. That was until Dr. Rice called. What a difference a day makes. My sister had warned me about becoming too emotional. "If you are hurt and angry," she said, "give no one the satisfaction of knowing; that's for when you call me."

"For God hath not given us the spirit of fear, but of power, and of love and of a sound mind."

There was that Bible verse again. It did not immediately quiet the sense of absolute letdown I was feeling, but it prevented me from feeling hopeless. Strangely, I did not feel sorry for myself. Anxious yes, but it seemed my mind and spirit were untouched by the back-to-back upheaval in my professional journey. It was as if God had reached down and covered me, so I did not lose my sense of self. I knew Ma-ma was praying. Her stubborn faith and single-minded belief system "that God had me" would not let me give in. She refused to let me be.

I stood up and left Dr. Lait's office. I did not return the chair in its spot. He was a stickler for returning chairs to their place, but I did not. It felt good. It even made me smile.

Six months later, while I was busy re-evaluating the next step of my educational journey, foreclosure proceedings were being filed on my fixer-upper house, and I was falling further behind in my car payment. Asking my mom to foot additional bills was out of the question. There was also a part of me that wanted to keep my problems hidden from the family, which was easy because I was far away from home. After days of much contemplation, deciding

THE LETTER

I had nothing to lose by trying, I picked up the phone. I had been laying low long enough. I did my praying. It was time to act.

"May I speak to your president?"

"May I ask who is calling?"

The voice on the other end, although perfected in its professional overture, was pleasant enough. I was placed on a brief hold during which I became nervous and unsure.

What would I tell the president of a bank? Would he or she listen or care? Would they grant my unusual request? I would have hung up out of fear, if my situation was not looking so grim. But when she came on the line and asked how she could help, I no longer felt afraid. Instead, I told Ms. McPherson in summary that I did not want my car repossessed.

"All the best in your journey," she responded rather kindly after listening patiently. "And in regard to the vehicle," she continued, "it will remain in your possession on the condition that you resume payments at the end of your medical training or before, if you're able."

It took a long while to process the unimaginable kindness that was extended to me by a stranger. Even today, as I share the story, it's hard to believe, because I am yet to find any similar story where, after over a year of making no payments on my car it was not repossessed. God is known for doing the impossible, the exceptional, and He worked it out so I would not have to worry about my car payment until I figured out my situation! I remained friends with Ms. McPherson and would intermittently call her to give updates. She became one of my biggest cheerleaders. Even today thoughts of her kindness still evoke in me a feeling of incredulity and thankfulness. In regards to the foreclosure process on my fixer-upper house, I averted a disastrous outcome within days of the final proceedings and sold the house.

My thankful sigh of relief could be heard around the globe once my car and my house situation was resolved. I would have danced with joy except I was still out of my medical training and had no clue what I was going to do with my life. It was not from lack of applications, nor from lack of knocking on doors. Rather, no program seemed interested in training me, and soon the months turned into a year. A slow realization was beginning to take root. Maybe there was no longer a path forward. Maybe that childish dream on the Hill with that letter written to God was a hoax. The soft voice that mocks a person's failure, the self-doubt that causes us to want to retreat, give up and become depressed—was no longer so soft. It was raging, loudly! I knew it was time to pray differently. I needed to pray in faith. If God had closed this door, then it was time to move. I just wished He would at least tell me why. Why bring me to the precipice and leave me there with seemingly nothing to hold on to?

Chapter 13

Deus Non Potest Percussum

"Deus non potest percussum" is Latin for "God cannot be beaten."

This phrase was once used in my hearing by a world-renowned obstetrician-gynecologist. He was the keynote speaker for the graduating seniors when I was in my first year at the former West Indies College. He was relentless in repeating that quote as he explained the challenges he had faced while undergoing medical training. He knows, performs, and teaches some of the most complex intrauterine surgical procedures in pregnant females, including blood transfusions while the fetus was still in the uterus, procedures that he helped perfect and was now teaching to the next generation of doctors.

Now, almost a decade later, *"Deus non potest percussum"* surfaced in my thoughts. Until then, that Latin phrase had left my memory; now though, it came roaring back. *"Deus non potest percussum."* Try as I might, I just could not shake the phrase from my mind. It was relentless, as if a voice was saying, "God cannot be beaten. Get up! God cannot be beaten." Through my tearless cries the same line was there, *"Deus non potest percussum* ... God cannot be beaten." Therefore, if God cannot be beaten and has a plan for my life, then it didn't matter if there were a thousand Dr. Rices. Her letter of discontent was of no consequence. God was on a warpath for me, but the battles were far from easy. I was rejected by two programs who had all but accepted me until Dr. Rice picked up the phone. I cannot tell you how many times I wished her away.

"That's not where God needed you," Ma-ma responded to my sigh of desperation. "Keep marching, one foot in front of the other."

"I will, but I can't keep this up. Pretty soon I will have no confidence in me or my abilities."

"Maybe that's what is supposed to happen to you, no confidence in self."

"Maybe, Ma-ma, but I can't seem to stop crying inside."

"Look ahead through the tears. The view is bigger there."

I felt Ma-ma's insistence was helped by not seeing the situation I was up against: their sophistication, their degrees, their influence. If she did, maybe she would have backed off a little and felt a tinge of intimidation, maybe. Knowing my Ma-ma, she would not have cared even after knowing; it would not have phased her.

Just when I thought that there were no more second-year residency positions available, and those that were available didn't seem interested, I was invited to attend two interviews. They were the last two remaining spots for the year 2006. For these final two interviews I decided on a different approach. Maybe Ma-ma was right; Dr. Rice was my "roadblock who was playing god with my future." I needed to step over or walk around it.

The day I showed up to my interview, I decided I would tell my story; after all, it was mine to tell, having lived the experience. In those interviews, I told my story down to every last detail, in vivid color; there was no apologetic slant to it either. I was done feeling afraid. I shut the door in the face of a roadblock that was threatening to engulf me. I explained how hard it was to keep going, knowing that someone of great influence and gravitas did not believe in me and was unwilling to give me the time I needed.

I described the difficulty in showing up for my daily rounds, the daily struggle of feeling unqualified to tell my patients and their loved ones, to not give up while I was fighting that feeling of anxious hopelessness myself. To ring the bell of surrender and to call it a day, agreeing that I didn't have what it takes would have seemed reasonable. While I told the interviewer my story, there was no avoiding it. I shared the faith that propelled me forward, the dream that I had to make a difference, to inspire and change at least one person in my lifetime in a massive way.

How could I not talk of a grandma who would not let me give up. I chose also to speak to the humanity in each of my interviewers. I knew like me, they or a person they love would face challenges to overcome. I spoke to that common humanity.

I finished my interview by somehow advocating the option of a choice: to choose to train me and to join the other attendings whose evaluations contradict that of Dr. Rice, a choice to help me prove her wrong. And when I was asked why, I responded by pointing to the files of letters from patients whose lives I had already managed to touch. After all, Dr. Rice's evaluation was not unanimous, not even close. There were more who believed in me. She just happened to be the one with the key to that door. I left the interviews knowing God had a plan for the rest of my journey. If I were no longer to be a medical doctor, it was because He knew best and I would be better off for it. I was ready to move on without looking back.

Two days later I had two letters of acceptance to finish my residence training. Thus, now my dilemma was no longer "if" I could finish, but rather which state I wanted to move to. I chose the training program that asked the hardest questions, the one that would be the most rigorous – the one that was willing to look more closely at me and rebuff the naysayer in the strongest terms. It was either sink or swim, to prove to myself and others that *"Deus non potest percussum,"* that failure can be proven as myth, and that the human spirit, when tied to God its Creator, can safely navigate and face with courage life's traumas and let downs, and carry its vision to reality.

Chapter 14

Love Never Ends

I opened my eyes to the most beautiful day imaginable. It took me a while to realize that I was not in Texas or Florida. I was home. The similarities of the places to where I recently sojourned deepened the confusion. The view from my bedroom window of the exotic blue sea, the cool breeze from the dancing tree branches tempering the spicy summer sun and the lazy loving feel of the surrounding was not unlike that of Galveston, Texas. There were, however, differences like the shameless rooster crowing in the distance, the loud barking of the untrained outdoor dogs, and the high-pitched squealing of the neighbor's pigs in the distance being marched off to the slaughter, soon to be someone's stew. All this interrupted my sweet slumber. No sense wishing for more sleep, I thought. It was Thursday; I was on the schedule for the diabetic care clinic. It had become routine that while on visits home, I would volunteer at the local clinics and the hospital. The hands-on experience was immensely helpful, and there was much less regulation. I was expected to see all sorts of issues in all age groups and come up with a reasonable diagnosis and care plan.

The difference in lack vs. abundance in my home country and that of my host training country could not be more noticeable. It was not uncommon to have the diagnosis but no treatment, or only part of what was needed.

THE LETTER

"What's the rest of your plans for the week?" Ma-ma asked as I brushed past her.

"I've signed up for more volunteer duties at the local clinic."

"I see."

"Will also be putting in a few hours for AJ in his seminars."

"I see." She sounded disappointed. It meant less time at home.

"But not every day, Ma-ma. I will be home most days."

"Glad that I am not forgotten."

A hit of melancholy was evident. I kissed her cheek, promising to return early. A tinge of guilt floated in my heart. I was home but not home, gone all day and coming home just before nightfall.

In truth, since my return, when not at the clinic, I had become almost a permanent fixture, accompanying AJ wherever he went. It was now our routine. AJ would arrive early in the morning; we'd drive as far as we could, and then trek the remainder of the way on foot to areas impossible to reach by car for his Bible studies and church services. I, on the other hand, would often be pulled into giving some sort of health seminar. They were pretty informal, but it was hard to ignore the signs and symptoms of undiagnosed diabetics and the other common health issues seen in developing countries, such as worm infestation, malnutrition, among others.

The families were mostly poor and lived off the land. Most had little to no running water, and not all the homes had electricity. Outdoor latrines were the norm for most families. Most of the youth who were fortunate enough to complete high school education opted to work in the city. In addition to our helping our indigent citizens in the rural hills, it also meant my spending more time with AJ. Oh joy! And though I had disagreed with Ma-ma who had on more than one occasion hinted that time with AJ was my major motivation for our missionary-like work, deep down I knew she was not entirely wrong.

"Diane Carol, your breakfast is getting cold!" Ma-ma called, pulling me out of my thoughts of the day ahead.

The diabetic specialist Dr. Joseph, whose clinic I was to spend the upcoming weeks working alongside, was considered the best in the area. His fame was so noteworthy that the story was making the rounds that he was able to not only treat and control the diabetics but cure the diabetes itself. It didn't matter that it was because of the aggressive weight loss program and dietary measures he insisted that all his patients follow, or else find care elsewhere. To his patients he was the miracle man.

On my first day, Dr. Joseph handed me a patient's chart. He proceeded to quickly introduce Mr. Rowe. His diagnosis was as anticipated: chronically uncontrolled blood sugar, resulting in poorly healing, recurrently infected foot wounds. A look of pity and a raised eyebrow was directed my way from Dr. Joseph's nurse. I was soon to learn why.

As I walked towards Mr. Rowe's room, he could be heard coughing. Possible COPD from his tobacco use, I thought. I entered his room and introduced myself. He was a cigarette smoker.

"A resident doctor in training?" he bellowed, eyeing me with suspicion.

"I will be seeing you, along with Dr. Joseph."

"Good. Then you can rescue me from that Dr. Joseph. He's trying to get me to give up real food and my cigar. I have no plans to."

His bluntness caught me off guard.

"We will address all your concerns," I said. "But, first, how are you feeling today?"

"With my hands," he responded, laughing loudly.

"Your chart stated that you have had some pain with swallowing. Has your swallowing improved?"

"I have been swallowing my pride all my life, so I would say my swallowing is just perfect." He erupted in another laughter, only this time even louder.

I lowered my eyes on his chart, not to read its contents, but rather to hide the uncertainty in my eyes. I had never experienced a patient of such demeanor. He found every question amusing. Every response he gave carried a hint of sarcasm or a pun. I looked to Dr. Joseph, hoping he would intervene. After all, he would know best how to handle the situation, but he was busy with his typing. And while I was sure he was aware of my ordeal (after all, Mr. Rowe's laughter rebounded from the wall, echoing through the office walls), his pretense of not hearing was admirable.

"Would you like help in quitting smoking?" I asked.

"No. All my friends who quit died shortly after. They may have lived longer if they hadn't. You see, their bodies grew accustomed to the smoke."

Mr. Rowe sounded so convinced that, if I didn't know the opposite to be true, he would have managed to convince me. He stared straight ahead as I explained to the contrary.

"I don't believe too much in your so-called 'medication,'" he answered matter-of-factly while hinting that he had no interest in a rebuttal. "You doctors don't know crap."

I tried to reason with Mr. Rowe, but he had no interest in cooperating. His belly laughs only grew louder, his puns and sarcasm more pointed. No longer having a belly laugh at my expense, he was in full passive-aggressive mode. This was the "break-out-in-a-sweat" patient interaction that I have long heard about. I tried every patient interview strategy taught, from open-ended questioning so that he could fill in the blanks at his comfort level, to the guided mono "yes," "no" response. But he was not interested.

After much internal debate, I formulated a plan and exited the room. It was time to see other patients. Mr. Rowe was offered the opportunity to wait for Dr. Joseph to see him, reschedule, or decide if this clinic is the best place for him to seek medical care. About half an hour later, I rejoined Mr. Rowe. His eyes held mine, daring me to look away. I didn't. It was now or never. This time he was ready, I hoped.

"I purposely gave you that patient," Dr. Joseph later explained, "knowing that he would test your ability to get the information you need and challenge your ability to stay on task. You will come across many a Mr. Rowe, and no textbook will prepare you. You have to figure it out, one patient at a time. You did fantastic. I could not have taught you how best to handle the situation."

I smiled brightly while inwardly sighing at the thought of "many a Mr. Rowe."

"Some patients," he continued, "will put up smoke screens, likely from fear, anger, and lack of trust. But never forget they come seeking your help, and so keep trying with patience. Most will eventually partner with you towards getting well."

"Thanks for the good advice."

"You have gotten more promises from Mr. Rowe in one visit than I have for the four years that he has been my patient. He is one of the few I can't seem to convince about anything medical. He seemed to have more confidence in what his buddies tells him about his diabetes."

I found Dr. Joseph's comments were encouraging, as I was still reeling from the elderly lady who dismissed me for not being a "real doctor," whom she had come to see, and told me I was too young to know my head from my feet, and asked me why I was not home learning to cook. Still, I found Dr. Joseph's patients were all fascinating, and all too soon, I was exiting his office for the last time and climbed into AJ's waiting car.

The usual, ever-present island rain slowed the drive home to a crawl. This did not help the unusually uncomfortable silence between us. AJ and I were returning from a rather long day's work and we were both extremely tired. But long days and tiredness were not new to either of us; thus, they could not explain the current mood. He also made it clear through nonverbal body language that he didn't want to entertain a conversation. I was keen to oblige, and except for the pitter-patter of the rain falling around us and the steady beat of the windshield wipers struggling against the water, it was silent.

"You okay?" I asked, remembering the time that we were halfway through our walk to his mission when he abruptly returned home. Unknown to him I had observed as he took quick puffs from an Albuterol inhaler. It was then that I realized he had asthma. He was having an unannounced acute asthma attack. We never spoke of it, then or after.

The rain carried on as if she had much work to be done and had fallen behind. It poured and poured and then poured some more. The downpour was filling up the poorly constructed drains, overflowing and flooding the roads. This was a constant on the island.

"Let me pull over," he said. "There is too much water to keep driving safely."

I usually would not mind the delay; it meant us spending more time together. But fatigue, my now constant companion, made me seconds away from falling asleep. I was also preoccupied with upcoming events. I was days away from singing at the youth crusade, and still had not chosen the songs and, worse, I was not inclined to practice. I was also on countdown to returning to the US to continue training. Both realities I wished I could postpone to a time of my liking.

Out of the corner of my eye, I sensed AJ staring at me and as I caught his eyes, his look was fathomless and sad. I held his gaze and wondered about the price of each other's calling. I, the doctor healer of the broken body; he, the minister healer of the broken life — each living out our portion of the age-old battle, the one that started with Adam and Eve, obedience to God vs. pleasing self, love of God vs. love of mammon, faith vs. doubt, godly purity vs. pleasure for a season.

Lately, the pain of separation had become more acute, the oppressive loneliness a harder burden to bear. Worn by the constant painful goodbyes, I was nevertheless totally in love with the man. I wished I could have it all at once.

"You're so quiet," he whispered.

"You're here. And this time, it's not a dream."

"Yes, here, take my hand," he offered as if sensing my struggles that maybe were his as well. The indescribable beauty in the simple act of holding another's hand ... awaking many emotions, offering ...comforts, love, restraints. So while holding my hand he reminded me, by way of paraphrasing Romans 8, to walk after the Spirit, preferring the things of God, of a Savior whose grace was enough for his children, and to know that nothing whatsoever can separate us from God's love. He finished by reminding me that I could do all things through Christ's strength ... including the hardship of separation.

At every turn, AJ chose godly leadership. His choices made it easier for me, for us, to choose obedience to God. And every time he chose God's way, I loved him even more. To honor him, to respect him—that's a vow I'd freely take, if God willed it. The rain finally eased up, enough to complete the drive home.

"Thank you," I said, forcing back a yawn of sheer fatigue as he helped me from the car. Holding my hands, he examined them as if seeing them for the first time.

"DC," his voice was hesitant and wistful. "DC, I am taking off. I won't be seeing you for the next few days."

"Where are you going?"

"I'll be around, but I need time alone for prayer."

I wanted to spend every waking hour with him, but his top priority was always developing a godly character, and for him that included spending uninterrupted time away from all else—me included, reading his Bible, praying and visiting whoever was in need of help from the church he assisted.

"I love you."

THE LETTER

"I love you totally." A goodnight hug, a quick smooch. I still believe God came up with the idea of a kiss and at its finest, it will always be divine and great. Just how He intended it. It didn't matter knowing Ma'ma was likely at her spy spot observing. I relished the moment.

Long after AJ's tail light had turned the corner, my face was still pressed against my window. I stood, staring into the distance. Nothing in particular had my focus, just my thoughts. I had grown accustomed to our praying about things together. This time he was doing it alone without me. "That's okay," I thought aloud, but those were only words.

Moments later, Bible in hand, I joined Ma-ma. It was time for evening prayer.

"How was your day?" She grunted without looking up, intent in her Bible reading.

"I will be going to the Hill for the next few days."

"Eeh," she muttered, eyes still focused on her Bible.

"Will be praying there for the next two days."

"Anything in particular?"

"No, I haven't decided yet. AJ will be praying alone for a few days, so I am following suit."

"Good idea. I imagine your new life can crowd out time for God, so use your off time well," she said, her eyes still intently scanning the Bible pages.

I must have fallen asleep while thinking about praying. My next conscious thought was the 7 am alarm clock chiming.

It had been almost a full week since AJ had taken off to pray. It was terrible, especially since my time to leave was drawing close. I missed him, feeling that he was near, but beyond my reach. I took comfort knowing that in a few hours, I would be seeing him at the youth evangelistic meeting, where he was scheduled to speak; I was slated to sing after he spoke.

"It's best we start getting ready," Ma-ma said, breaking into my thoughts.

"We still have time. It's 5:00 and the program starts at 7:00."

"Not by my standard," Ma-ma retorted.

Arriving late to any event was at the top of her "avoid-at-all-times" list, especially events related to church. I was about to mount another argument of having more than enough time when the doorbell rang. It was AJ.

I overheard him telling Ma-ma that he was there to take me to the youth meetings. I was somewhat relieved for Ma-ma; she hated driving at night and was not keen on attending the youth program. She found it too "lively," her way of saying, "loud and bordering irreverent." AJ's coming had spared her. I was also happy for me: finally, time together with AJ, after his week hiatus! Hoping to impress him some, I took extra care in my dressing. I liked the result and hoped he would notice.

"Ready?" he asked upon entering the room.

"Let's walk a bit. We have time." He headed toward the exit, and I followed.

Not long into the walk AJ announced, "DC, I think God wants us to go our separate ways. I have been praying for months and this is the decision He has led me to."

I glanced at his face. Undefinable emotions captured his expression. His brown eyes were joyless.

No tears, no pleading words escaped my lips, just a sense of disbelief. I had no inkling. It was all so unexpected. His look was haunting, waiting for my response. We kept walking. The once beautiful night sky suddenly looked gray and colorless. The silence between us grew.

"Go our separate ways? What way would that be, after walking so closely together? Our journey has been perfect. Our dreams are one and the same."

"Some things are impossible to imagine, except when seen through God's eyes."

"You said that this is where He has led you, so then there is nothing for me to do but to accept."

But those were words. What I felt was different. I took on sadness in a way that was unimaginable. It would have helped to cry, but I knew if I started, there would be no stopping, and the evangelistic meeting was about to start. I felt like asking him to wait, to pray more. I wondered if he was sure. I did not want to make it hard for him to follow through on God's leading as he perceived it. Even though I desperately wanted to ask him to reconsider, I did not.

"This cannot be easy for him," I thought. I had no reason to believe it was. I never doubted His love for me, but I always knew he would follow God's leading above all else. After praying so earnestly that he would be for me and I for him, it never occurred to me that God's will could be different.

On our way to the event, we managed an unnatural lighthearted conversation, the contents of which I have no memory. We both knew it was not the time to let how we truly felt or wanted give sway. We always knew we would only want for each other what God wanted for us. And for now, it was each going our separate paths.

That night, at the evangelistic meeting AJ stuck to his script. His topic was something about full commitment to Christ. How fitting for him, I thought. For a brief moment, I regretted not having my own car. That may have been the moment when I would have snuck off, hid in my car and cried myself into nothingness. He was so serious in his bearing, to the point of looking sad.

While those around me were praying, singing, and finding enjoyment in full worship, I was preparing my heart to accept a loss yet to be defined. When I sang the pre-chosen hymn of invitation to the altar for prayer, "I Surrender All," by Windfield Scott Weeden, I wondered if I should trust and surrender all to a God who seemed to allow such a rough path for me.

When the meeting was over, we were the first to exit the sanctuary. As was his custom, he held the car door for me to climb in. Some events can only be faced in silence. This, for me, was one. We drove in silence. I remember him glancing at me only once, after which his eyes remained glued to the road as he drove me home. Arriving, I headed to my room, knowing I had to keep moving. Hours later, suitcase packed, I knocked on Ma-ma's door.

"How was the meeting?" she asked. Luckily her eyes were closed; otherwise she would have known.

"I have to get back to my training. I'm leaving tomorrow at dawn."

"Tomorrow, why so sudden?"

"Something important came up."

"Is everything ok?"

I could not breathe, much less speak. Of course, everything was not okay. Soon AJ was to be a memory.

"Must be important. What is it?"

"I have to leave sooner. Duty calls," was all I could muster. Another day in AJ's town without him? That I could not bear.

"You have spoken to AJ, I assume?"

I struggled. I wanted to tell Ma-ma but I did not want to crumple before her. She would have comforted me as I wept, broken and inconsolable, but I couldn't bear her seeing me so utterly undone. I already knew the advice that she would offer. She'd remind me of how God's plan for my life is best and to leave my future in His hands. She had a sixth sense about things. I could not help but wonder if she had already sensed AJ's struggle, if she'd seen this coming. I hugged her without answering her questions.

"Pray for me, Ma-ma."

"I always do."

THE LETTER

"Pray a bit more." I hastily bade her goodnight and hurried to my room.

Alone, I lay on my bed and stared at the ceiling. Sleep eluded me. I tried praying, but the words mocked me. My thoughts reproached me. I felt lost and rejected. God must have found me unworthy. I thought my path would have been easier. We were perfect together. Of that I was sure. Now I had nothing to hold onto. Self was at a low ebb.

"God, have I not walked before You with a humble heart? Is there nothing good in me? I have sought Your will in all things. I have always loved You best, keeping myself for Your glory, yet the one thing I asked—You denied? For years I have prayed. What have I done to deserve this?"

Like Job, like Jacob, like one who has suffered a great loss, I spent the entire night justifying, bargaining, reliving, promising, recommending, pleading. I just could not let go.

I watched from my window. The day was breaking on the horizon. It was time for me to leave. The taxi horn announced its arrival. I quietly crept down the flight of stairs. Ma-ma was still asleep. It was still quite early so I decided to let her be. Instinctively, and out of habit, I knelt beside her bed, resting my head beside her still frame. She placed her hand on my head. All the while, she slept.

"Love you, Ma-ma." Kissing her forehead, I took one final look around. Everything looked the same. Yet, everything had changed. This place would now hold a memory of sadness.

I opened the door and hurried toward the cab. A cold wind hit my face. Unprepared, I had forgotten how chilly the Island mornings can be. It felt more so now, maybe a reflection of my heart.

I arrived a week and a half ahead of my scheduled return to my residency training. As news of my early arrival spread among the hospital staff, commending words and high fives came my way. A few junior doctors wanted to know if I had lost my right mind. If only they knew that I was a runaway.

My new residency director, who had taken a keen interest in my medical training, thought I was a "superstar." After all, how many doctors in training gave up vacation to come back to hard work? Internship and residency is known for what it was: challenging, long, and tough. So, to volunteer for extra time of hard labor was unheard of. But after the breakup, I had nowhere to go, nothing to do, except to return to training. Once I arrived, I had no desire to be there, no motivation to study, no strength to work.

For a very long time, being paged to the telephone or a letter's arrival would make my heart stop. Hope would surge. But that was all it was, a racing heart powered by false hope. There were to be no letters, no phone calls, no attempted communication from either side.

How did I survive? Work, and in addition to my assignments, I became the permanent volunteer for anyone needing extra help. I studied obsessively, days on end, sleeping and eating enough only to survive. It left me no time to ponder anything else. When it was time to take my next in-training exam, I was fearless. When I accepted the award for the highest score for two consecutive years, and most improved trainee, and harnessed the best peer evaluation from interns and those senior, I could not help but wonder if it all was worth the price.

"Dr. DC, please call the OR."

I groaned a bit louder than I intended. As usual I found it irritating and unwelcome, the overhead page at such early morning. Such a page, especially to the operating room, usually indicated urgency. The smoothness of the operator, a well-trained professional voice, could not hide from me, the doctor, the reality to which I had been called. Urgency in medicine, and so much more so in surgery, is never a good sign. Someone is dying, and, with God's help, we were there to prevent it. Also, such an early morning page easily set the tone for the entire day, a day full of adrenaline rush. Stressful. Demanding. Stretching one's limits to the maximum, to the breaking point. But I held onto a thread of hope that my being called to the OR was a mistake and it was meant for Dr. Sanchez. He was the surgical resident for the month, and he was on call to the OR. I was on an elective surgical rotation, an elective I opted to do and today I was assigned to the surgical floor. The surgical floor for me meant less caseload and a more predictable routine, a welcome relief. If things went as planned for once, I had the real possibility of getting out before nightfall. In contrast, the OR was hard to reconcile its one moment of surreal calmness to the other of unbelievable hyperactivity brought on by a horrific accident or a routine procedure that suddenly turns bad. I gingerly picked up the phone.

"Please come to the OR at once."

No greeting. No pleasantries. Just the order. Dr. Smith's voice, the attending plastic surgeon, sounded terse. I ran the flight of stairs to the OR. The elevator was too slow.

"Hurry and scrub in," he said. "The surgical resident is out sick. I have called in for help, but won't be here for another hour at the most. I have a long day ahead and any delay can complicate the schedule, so I need you to fill in for now."

All that was said in one breath. All the time Dr. Smith was busy scrubbing and gowning to start the operation. I groaned inwardly, but he could not tell from the well-practiced, glad-to-help smile I offered.

The surgery in question was a facelift, a no-rush procedure where the sagging wrinkled facial skin, a telltale sign of aging, would be carefully separated, nipped, cut, tossed, repositioned, and sutured, all in one scoop in an attempt to reverse, at least to some degree and temporarily, the patient's age. Hours later, I was still holding the surgical separators, mopping up blood, and cauterizing bleeding arteries. I was used to long hours, but not to standing and holding my arms in one spot for what seemed like forever. I was exhausted and could not feel my feet.

"We're almost done," said Dr. Smith, as he stepped back examining the now silicone augmented lips.

Moments later, I stumbled into the doctor's quarters, falling onto one of its empty beds. Except for removing my white coat, I snuggled into the covers, fully dressed with my shoe-clad feet dangling over the edges. I was afraid that I would fall asleep if I made myself comfortable. All I needed was ten minutes of debrief. My day was far from over.

"Please, don't fall asleep," I warned myself. "You still have to round on the post-op patients."

I could hear indistinguishable chatter and footsteps hurrying back and forth in the corridor below my window. No warning given, the door flung open. I half opened my eyes just in time to see one of the cardiology fellows quickly grab a notebook and rush out.

Intent on getting my minutes, I again settled into the covers and closed my eyes when a scene floated in my consciousness: I was dreaming, except I was still awake. It was AJ. He was lying alone in a hospital bed, gravely ill. I noticed a nebulous figure waiting beside him. As I drew closer, I caught sight of both arms stretched towards me. In one hand, he held a beautiful wedding gown. I instinctively wondered to whom it belonged. But his other hand caught my eyes to where he had a doctor's coat. It was so plain, unattractive, no match for the beauty of the wedding gown but it was sparkling clean and neatly pressed.

"AJ is sick and dying," the nebulous figure spoke. "You love him much, but your only chance of marrying him is now." He continued handing me the gown. I hesitated.

"He is too sick to make a decision to the contrary. He will marry you."

THE LETTER

"What of the coat?" I asked. "If you choose the coat, then you become his doctor. With your care he may survive but he will never marry you." I slowly began to understand. "You will have to choose one."

But how can I choose where there has never been a choice?

Once you love someone it never stops. Love never ends. It only changes and adapts to its reality. AJ believed God had separate paths for us. Hidden away in my heart, the story was different. For me it was just a matter of finishing my training and going home to continue where we left off, always praying it would be God's will. But now, in what seemed like a sleep-wake trance, I was asked to let go of that prayer – to choose.

I turned toward my patient. The white coat was draped around my shoulder.

"Dr. Vanhorne, please call the operator." I sat up with a start, breaking out in a sweat. The scene was all too vivid. It was like a vision. And yet it had been four years since I had any contact with AJ. I felt confused.

"Dr. Vanhorne, please call the operator." Again, that smooth voice. It always irritated me. Its smoothness hid the status of the situation to which I was called. I could be called to the most warzone-like situation in the ER, with patients fighting for their lives left, right, and center, and the operator's voice would still make it sound like she was alerting me to an invitation to sit in a garden and observe the water fountain, my favorite drink in hand.

I lifted the phone. "Hello, this is Dr. VanHorne."

"Hold for a call." A second later, "Go ahead. You're connected."

"Hello?"

"DC, this is Karen. I have been trying to find you for a week." Her voice was low and hesitant, as if searching for the right words.

"I lost my brother." A long pause followed. Karen had two brothers, but I instantly knew which one. God had prepared me for the news.

"AJ died suddenly from an asthma attack," she continued.

To see him one last time, even from a distance—would never be.

"He didn't forget you. Your pictures are still to be found in his album. You can take what you wish. He kept your birthdate. It was the combination that gave me access to the briefcase where he kept his personal documents." She continued into the silence. He had moved on, but I was not forgotten. I took comfort in the Bible's promise of the resurrection.

"Only God knows the end of all things," Ma-ma would often state. "Only God knows tomorrow."

AJ and I were only allowed to start the journey together. He completed his mission as healer of the broken lives. A pastor, rather a minister of the gospel of Jesus Christ, a preacher, a man of God, as he often styled himself. I am to continue mine as healer of the broken bodies, as a medical doctor.

I reached for my white coat; it hung on my thin frame. Securing its buttons, I walked briskly along the long, cold corridor to the surgical ward. The ambulances were busy arriving and leaving, their sirens blasting, always so loud and ominous, sounding urgent. Some days I hated them. Today was not one. They rather confirmed the reality I was to live.

Chapter 15

The Interview

Soon, I took another 30-second walk and was handed another certificate, this time certifying that I had successfully completed my specialty training in internal medicine. Weeks later, I took the medical board exams, passed, and became a diplomate in internal medicine. That meant I could now work as a board-certified medical doctor in the area of internal medicine.

I did just that, taking my first job offer at a Hospital in Alamogordo, New Mexico. But it was not long before a feeling of despair and unsettledness hung over my everyday routine. I was experiencing a sadness unknown to me, close to depression.

Loida felt I had never taken the time needed to mourn and live the losses I encountered along the way. She felt I had just been sweeping things under the proverbial carpet in order to keep moving on. I found myself praying earnestly for peace and a way forward. I longed for peace and assurance.

The more I prayed, the more stuck I felt. I signed the work contract for three years and could not breach its terms. My conscience would not let me. There were provisions of buying out the remaining time. It was calculated to be in the hundreds of thousands of dollars and I did not have hundreds of thousands of dollars. I continued to pray, asking my home church to pray as well. Six months later, an unexpected breakthrough came.

THE LETTER

During my final year of training in internal medicine, I took a special interest in the area of infectious diseases and considered pursuing a subspecialty in that field. The competition was fierce; sometimes as many as one hundred candidates vied for one spot.

I was informed of an opening at the University of Florida's Shands Hospital, with co-training in the area of transplant infection at the Mayo Clinic. "An easy move from New Mexico to Florida," I concluded. I was invited to apply. I did and was straight away accepted. I believe God truly understands and is intimately involved in the human condition. He opened doors that may have been otherwise closed to me. He met me even at the level of my emotions.

As for the contract stipulation, Mr. Howard, the CEO, was more than gracious. He was like a soothing instrument. He smoothed the way for the hospital board to release me from all the contractual stipulations. "Go get your subspecialty. I would want the same for my son," were his parting words.

The background to all this was that Mr. Howard and I had bonded over a shared commonality: his son was now on the journey to becoming a medical doctor. As a result, whenever I crossed paths with the CEO, bursting with pride, he would make it a habit of eagerly sharing stories of his boy's "amazing bone repairs" as he put it. He would at times repeat the same stories, only adding a few more lines. The problem? He was never in a hurry; I always was. The CEO would basically carry on a long one-sided conversation, proudly touting his son's success as an orthopedic doctor in training. "I'll just call him a bone carpenter," he conceded, laughing after a rather long story.

Inwardly, I was in a rush to get on to my next patient; outwardly, I was all ears, smiling and nodding appropriately; after all, he was my boss. Looking back, I'm glad I gave him time that I didn't have. In turn, he gave me the time I needed to move on. Freed from my contract, I quickly made the move to Florida. I immediately felt at peace believing this was the next step God would have me make. On to further medical training--to subspecialize in the area of infectious diseases.

Everything was going according to plan . . . until Ma-ma called.

"When will you come see me?" were her first words.

"Soon, Ma-ma."

"It has been years. How many?" she asked, as if forcing me to acknowledge the number of years since I had last been home. "I am still here."

Her voice and words moved my heart to tears, but my mind was unmoved. I had not been back, at least physically, since I rested my head on her lap that morning I left. Despite her many entreating words, and my having been relentlessly haunted by memories of home, she still had failed in her efforts to get me back. I was truthful when I told Ma-ma I was busy. But she and I knew that I would never be too busy to come home.

"I pray that I will see you before I die," she said with hope in her voice.

"You will."

By the time we ended the call I was close to tears. This woman whom I adored, who raised me, who once I obeyed without question, had not lost all influence over me. That night I had a fitful sleep and as a result I woke up late.

I was rushing toward the medical intensive care unit to begin the day's rounds as an Infectious Diseases Fellow, when I was called to the Medical Director's office. To be called this early and told to come at once because another fellow (a doctor in subspecialty training) was assigned to assume my duties signaled that this meeting was not only gravely important, but a decision had already been made. A sense of foreboding echoed from each footstep that carried me closer to the office. As I entered the Director's office, I noticed that the senior fellow was waiting along with the program director; the coordinator was there, ready to take notes. On display, an open letter rested on

THE LETTER

top of a folder with my name boldly written in black. Their solemn expression did nothing to alleviate my anxiety.

Not again, Lord. I can't do this again. Memories of my intern year, when I was told that I would not make it, washed over me. I could hear, in my own ears, my heart pounding. I sent up a quick prayer.

"Thank you for coming at such short notice," the director said, trying to smile as she motioned for me to take a seat. The smile, however, was quickly replaced by a look of concern.

"We received this letter from immigration services." She handed me the letter. I tried, but failed, to control the tremor in my hand.

"They are requesting you go back home to be re-interviewed at the US embassy. Your training is immediately suspended, pending the interview."

"Interview? Why? Did they say why?"

"No," she responded.

"When?"

"Today, if you can get a flight out."

"And after the interview?"

"If the immigration officer conducting the interview is satisfied," she said, "you will be allowed back into the US to continue your training."

It took me a while to fully grasp the implication of the situation. It was at the interviewer's discretion. It had been a long time since I prayed with such desperation. My entire future flashed before me.

"God, I am tired. It's enough. What else? How much more? Lord, be gentle with me, for I am but a human, a woman young and frail."

I took the short drive from the hospital back to my apartment. A tiny laughter of hysteria tried to capture the moment:

"Oh, Lord, I need to go see Ma-ma, but You didn't have to involve the government."

The words of Jeremiah which I had read so often, came to mind. "I know, Lord, that we humans are not in control of our own lives,"

THE INTERVIEW

Hours later I touched down in Jamaica's capital, Kingston. I headed directly to the American embassy.

"No, ma'am, you will not see the consulate today. You have no appointment," the guard at the embassy gate sternly informed me. He swelled with pride at his own importance. All who came, some desperately, must pass through him—and he knew it.

"Can I make the appointment now?"

"They are made online, on our website. There are no same day appointments, so the earliest appointment is likely months away."

"But I have to get back to my training."

"I did not make the rules, ma'am," he answered, and with that, called for the next person in line.

I turned away, reluctantly, my heart heavy, my spirit bruised. The idea of not being allowed back to complete my fellowship training was beginning to seem a real possibility. I must trust God. He knows the whys and the outcome. I tried to reassure myself, but in all truth, I was panicking. My stomach was burning as it always does when I'm under great stress. What would become of me now?

Karen, AJ's sister, and I spent the evening filling out the online application. The appointments were booked out several weeks ahead. It did not take me long before I realized that I would lose the training spot unless something miraculous happened.

A scene from the Hill flooded my mind. The letter I wrote to God–He who faithfully opened every door while I was in medical school, my internship, and residency, the same God who had helped me along, answered my every feeble request for His name's sake is the same God now. The memory of God prompted me to call Librada, my friend, prayer partner and mentor. She was in her early seventies, a retired nurse who now spent her time praying for others.

"I will pray, and I will put calls out to my prayer group, and we will meet in the evening to continue in prayer for you," she reassured me. "I will put your situation at the level of intensive care," she stated, her way of saying she understood the seriousness of my situation. "Meanwhile, go do what you need to do while we here will pray."

The moment I hung up the phone with Mrs. Librada, I felt impressed to call the US Council office in Washington. The female voice on the other end sounded pleasant enough. I explained my dilemma.

"There is nothing that I can do. We are not in control of the local embassy appointments," she informed me, but not without compassion in her voice.

"If you were able, would you help me?" I asked pointedly. A pause followed.

"I will speak to my supervisor. One moment, please."

The word "supervisor" produced such a relief that, without thinking, I hung up the phone for a happy dance. I quickly redialed; it rang unanswered. The next day I was back at the embassy gate. The same guard was there; his expression was serious and business-like. I still did not have an appointment for that day, but somehow, I made my way past the guard and made a beeline towards the ambassador's office. The guard was in hot pursuit, but I was undeterred.

"Ma'am, I told you yesterday that you are not allowed on embassy property without an appointment."

I kept going.

"Miss, stop right now. I can arrest you at a minimum," he scolded. I was aware of the gun on his hip, his hand hovering. Maybe out of custom, I was not afraid. Part of me knew he would not harm me.

"Please, I need to get back to school. Will you help me?" He had now caught up and was in lockstep.

"Okay, come."

A few minutes later, the guard stood before his supervisor with me next to him.

"She already has her approved student documents and is here only to be re-interviewed. It's just protocol, but her documents are in order," the guard informed his supervisor, a woman. Strange that

THE INTERVIEW

he was now my advocate trying to justify my presence at the US embassy under such conditions. I remained quiet and allowed him to make the case; after all, he was the one with the embassy uniform and identification. If anyone could legitimize my plight and why I should be helped, that would be him.

"What is the name? Does she have an appointment? She will need an appointment," the supervisor continued.

"No appointment," the guard responded apologetically.

"What do you expect me to do?"

She made no attempt to hide her surprise, all the while she kept reviewing the appointment log. "What did you say her name was?"

I spoke up, giving my name.

"Her name was added on as an emergency case from a directive higher up," she stated, turning to the guard.

"Yahweh, you're awesomeness, and I love you for it!" I mouthed. I was sure it was done by Washington DC. For me, this further brought home Proverbs 21:1: "The Lord controls rulers, just as he determines the course of rivers" (CEV).

The guard eyed me suspiciously as he walked back to his post, but I didn't let it bother me a bit. In a few minutes I would face my interviewer.

The interviewer was professional and relentless. Unsmiling. My every move, all my activities while in her beloved homeland were open for her to see. I prayed while answering her questions. Then she asked about my medical training. That was the only easy question, and I took it. I discussed my involvement in research, my love for medicine, my hope to be a missionary, and my desire to make a difference. In that moment, I became acutely aware of blessings and opportunities that I may have taken for granted.

With nothing more to add, and without forethought, I asked my interviewer about her home; her accent sounded Texan, a lot like Dr. Rice, almost. That was the only time I saw what seemed like a flicker of a smile cross her face. The human experience is often shared. Like me, she was young, away from home, and diligent at her task — likely missing her home and adapting to a new culture. Possibly, as I had, she lost loved ones while away.

"When are you due back to your training?" she asked, deflecting my question.

"Since I arrived three days ago."

She stamped my form "Approved!"

"Here you go, and good luck."

She quickly moved on to her next case, but not before I noticed a flicker of emotion in her eyes. She knew her decision had impacted my life forever. For good.

"God, You are 'awesomeness'! Thank You."

As I exited the embassy gate, I tried thanking the security guard. He was not interested. Maybe he was still reeling from my determined defiance. I thanked him anyway and hurriedly exited the embassy compounds. Karen, AJ's sister was waiting. Her joy was equal to mine.

The very same day, I took the next flight out to Miami, and from there made my way to Jacksonville. I left the airport and headed directly to the hospital to report for duty. On my way in, I crossed paths with the senior fellow coming off night shift, my shift. He stood in the gap for me. He raised his hand over his head in an applause sign.

"Still standing?" he asked, smiling.

"Still standing," I responded all the while hurrying towards the hospital, directly to the ICU to accept the patient who would be under my care.

I was still standing. God was standing with me!

Chapter 16

Creator vs. Darwin

I was happy to finally have a complete day off after working twelve days in a row to make up for time lost attending the legendary interview. I was happier yet to be alone. A sandwich, my daily devotional book, a Bible, and a notepad were my only companions. This was my "do-nothing" day, and I intended to spend most, if not all, of it at the park. After a bit of looking, I hastily claimed the farthest seemingly most secluded spot in the park and made myself comfortable. I thought, "rest at last," except that a dog who had escaped its owner was feverishly sniffing my belongings.

"Leave me alone," I ordered through partially closed eyes. "Go away," I whispered through clenched teeth and a discrete stern look, hoping not to upset the owner who maybe was observing.

It's not that I don't love dogs. It was timing. I myself was once a pet owner. My dearly beloved cat, Jellybean, would testify to that fact. He took off, never again to be seen the day that I left home for medical school. My pet goat, called Gellybeen, did not fare any better. According to the report that Ma-ma gave me, Gellybeen had been stolen and made into a stew shortly after I left home. I decided not to have any more pets unless I could provide a permanent home and watch over them myself, none of which was an option anytime soon. The dog neared my face, wagging his tail with an outstretched tongue coming in for a kiss. I sat up, quickly missing its wet smooch by seconds. But the dog would not be outdone and was closing in for a second try.

"Burt, come over here." That must be the owner walking towards me. It was a speckled pre-teen face; her eyes spoke a million apologies.

"Hey, Dr. Vanhorne," she greeted me.

"You know my name?" I asked, surprised. "I never made your acquaintance."

"You're in the same hospital with my brother. He's over there." As she pointed, my eyes followed. I recognized him instantly. Dr. Lucas, ophthalmology fellow, self-proclaimed agnostic and flirting with Darwinism.

"I am astounded that any true scientist could believe in the Creation story."

"The Big Bang," I responded, "sounds more incredible to me. I am baffled that you a doctor could look at the miracle of conception, the complexity of one cell, the amazing structure of the DNA of a strain of hair, and not believe it was created by design."

That day, after long point-by-point discussion, we agreed to call a temporary truce while challenging each other to re-evaluate our respective positions. That exchange was a little over a month before. Now there he was walking toward me as self-assured as one would expect from a first-generation cum laude graduate.

I hope he'll get his dog and move along, I reasoned silently, not at all enthused at his rapid approaching presence. He may be ready for another creation-evolution debate, but I was oh too tired.

"Hi." He extended his hand in greeting.

I eyed him warily, and then said: "My hand is still evolving. I'm afraid if I shake your hand, it may explode and fall off, morphing into a cow." I watched as his eyes flickered, not quite sure if he should laugh or debate the point. I left his hand hanging a bit more before I smiled. He followed suit.

"How are you?" he asked, sounding relieved.

"Actually, I have been wondering about the eye, and since you are the expert, why don't you sit and answer a few questions for me?" I invited him before I could stop myself.

He jumped at the opportunity, and without my permission before I could protest, he retrieved my notebook and pen and was feverishly drawing the anatomy of the normal eye. Without pausing to breathe, he explained with in-depth knowledge and enthusiasm the normal eye before carefully pointing out the areas of likely disease and the solutions that he often offered to his patients.

"And all human eyes carry the same information, and perform the same function, no matter the color. As if created by a master design …" The latter part he finished in a hushed tone of silence as if speaking to himself. His expression was fathomless, as if something great was just revealed to him for the first time.

Not known for not having a ready word when it comes to a biblical debate, I was speechless. Fearful that I might have interrupted whatever was going on in his thought processes, I remained silent. In the past, all my talk of a Creator, a master designer, was soundly and summarily dismissed by him. I was treated as unlearned and pitied for being simple-minded.

Maybe now it was to be the work of the Holy Spirit? Maybe my work with him was done, no more debating needed, the expounding of Scripture unnecessary.

"DC, what do you want to tell me today?" Lucas asked looking squarely at me, his demeanor was strangely and openly inviting.

"Well, we can start at the beginning with the book of Genesis 'In the beginning God created,' and then work our way to the book of John 'For God so loved…'" When Lucas did not refuse or argue the point, I continued. He listened politely but asked no follow-up questions. It was hard to read the moment, but I continued, often praying in my mind.

Twenty minutes into the conversation, Lucas' sister said, "I am hungry," and tugged at his arm. Her park playmate was gone, so she sought out her brother.

We said our goodbyes, but not before Lucas promised to continue the conversation.

Well, Lord, I did as you asked me and explained to Lucas Your work of creation and redemption. It's back over to You, so can I go back to my rest. Can I get some alone time?

It was to be four months later that I again found myself in the company of Dr. Lucas. We were participating in the care of a mutual patient, Mr. Paul, who was considered one of the hospital's "Frequent Flyers." It seemed that he was admitted on a monthly basis, if not more frequently. He was loved by the staff, in no small part due to his positive attitude. He never complained about what could be easily accepted as a difficult life. At age 26, he underwent a heart transplant after he suffered total heart failure. While the transplant was successful, the complications he suffered were many and varied: multiple infections and total kidney failure placed him on hemodialysis.

"All I had was the flu, but it totally destroyed my heart," he lamented. "After being told that I needed a new heart, I gave up on life itself. It wasn't like I could run down to the clothing store and get one. I all but banned my family from visiting and almost renounced my faith … saying the name 'Jesus' was the only prayer I could muster, repeating it over and over in my head. But here I am, sixteen years later, often wondering who died so I could have his heart and live."

I was still listening to Paul's story, the one he repeated on every hospital admission that we all pretended we were hearing for the very first time, when Dr. Lucas entered the room and began his assessment of Mr. Paul's vision. After what seemed like but a few seconds, he presented the diagnosis and described his plan of care.

"On to the next patient I go," he stated, and then said, "But I do have follow-up questions about our last discussion on the Genesis creation."

Though I had been praying for the same opportunity to continue, I was surprised at the request. I recovered in time to offer the next day at lunch time. I broke my promise to my sister not to discuss the creation story at work.

Without further delay, I bid him a "good day." Moving on to the next patient was my highest priority. As I entered Ms. Veronica's room, my hope was that she would be less chatty than her usual self. I was beginning to fall behind in the schedule and hoped to stay laser focused to get my work done with no small talk.

"I am a grandmother now," she said proudly. As I entered her room, she was desperately trying to sit up in bed. She was completely bed-ridden and wheelchair dependent. Her profound weakness was brought on by the ravages of multiple sclerosis, and at the young age of 24 was confined to a wheelchair.

"Linda gave birth to three healthy babies, a boy and two girls," she continued, handing me pictures of the new arrivals. I sat on the bed enjoying the moment with her. Linda turned out to be a dog that she had acquired 6 months ago.

"Tell me," I asked, handing her back the pictures, "what's the one thing you would have changed about your life?" I knew she was about to say being able to walk, or that there would be a cure for multiple sclerosis in her lifetime.

"Finish high school," she responded without a moment of hesitation. Her voice trailed softly. "Every beginning of the school year, my mom and I would head off to a great start, the excitement of the first day of school." Her voice mirrored the emotions she must have felt back then. "But, as the school year progressed, it would prove too much. The flu, the pain, the weakness, the infections, one followed the other. I was in the hospital for weeks on end. The lost time became too much, and I just kept falling behind." Her eyes teared up. "I just could not catch up. But I tried, I did try," she said brightly as if to cheer herself up. "Every year I was there," she reminisced. "Every year I showed up." She finished.

Our mutual silence hung in the room.

"That's the only thing I would change," she repeated.

I reached for her hand. That's all I could do, and often too many times that was the best I felt I could do as a physician.

Chapter 17

My Final 30-Second Walk

Five years of medical school, one transitional year of Family Practice, an intern year in Pediatric and Internal Medicine, three years of Internal Medicine residency, and three years of Infectious Disease Fellowship training, in that order. Again, here I was getting ready to take another 30-second walk. This one was to be the final walk. This time, I would be handed a certificate saying that I was now a diplomate in the sub-specialty area of infectious diseases. I would be considered one of the lead authorities in that field of study.

But that half-minute walk I would take only after having sat for the infamous exit interview. There, the Dean of Medicine, chief of departments, and the fellowship program directors would offer their input relating to my fellowship training and my worthiness, or unworthiness, to have the hand of fellowship extended to me.

Though told by my peers that the exit interview was usually a mere formality, just a congratulatory you've-made-it moment, I was nervous. Ready or not, the day of the interview arrived just like any other day. No family accompanied me, no red carpet, no one to hold the door open, and no drum roll. It was just an ordinary sunny day in Florida. There was only one thing that was outside of the ordinary. I was especially early. Tardiness had been a real struggle throughout my journey. I was about to alight from my car

THE LETTER

and begin the walk toward the Dean's office when an invisible hand on my shoulder restrained me.

"Pray before you walk in there," I was admonished. The impression was undeniably strong and so, reluctantly, I eased back into my car. With a one-second prayer now out of the way I was about to leap from the car when, again, I was restrained. This time I settled in.

"Ok, Father, here I am." Only after I felt the peace in doing so did I exit my car and purposefully make my way toward the interview. As I neared the Director's office, I overheard my name being called and it arrested my stride.

"No, I will not sign off on her recommendation." The voice was resolute.

"But it's customary. Every other fellow before her was given the opportunity." The other voice sounded somewhat sympathetic, though her tone registered unease. "Without your signature, she will not be able to take the medical board exam."

"She will not be able to," his voice confirmed without a hint of sympathy.

"Will you at least authorize the funds for a board review. Every fellow before was granted those funds, and at minimum it will increase her chance of passing the exam?"

"It will not make a difference. I am confident that she will not pass the exams. That money will be diverted elsewhere. I'll think of something."

Dr. Sanders was recently promoted to Professor of Medicine, the highest achievement in his field. His words now, more than ever, carried unchallenged authority. The wind behind his back, he was notably still basking in the admiration and congratulations of his colleagues. "Hail to the chief" was still heard as he walked, quiet, tall and stately along the great halls of the hospital with his entourage of fearful students, interns, residents and fellows. In addition to his professorship, Dr. Sanders accumulated more than forty years experience training doctors, many of those years not only in general Internal Medicine but in the subspecialty area of Infectious Diseases, as Program Director. He was, therefore, uniquely positioned to render an evaluation on any doctor in training. I would not be allowed to sit for the prestigious medical boards in infectious diseases was his evaluation.

My body became tense as I stood in the hallway, listening. It seemed like only yesterday when this selfsame professor had chosen me, his handpicked fellow, to join the program that he led, for the year 2010. I would carry the torch upon his retirement. But now he was refusing to recommend me for the prestigious specialty board exams?

The conversation continued after a momentary pause; his words were like arrows landing on its target with devastating precision. Dr. Sanders' voice, though low-pitched, was unhesitating; each word spoken was unbuffered with kindness, not carrying a glimmer of hope to my listening ear. Tears stung my eyes as I realized that they were speaking about me. Only the conversation was not intended for my listening ears.

As I stood there stunned, I reflected on the day that I called his program and expressed my interest, requesting additional information. The following day the chief himself called to conduct a pre-screen interview, followed by a formal face-to-face sit down interview with him and his staff.

On the day of the interview he said: "Tell me, in one sentence, why you took a year before applying for this fellowship?"

His question was reasonable: over ninety percent of doctors do their subspecialties following completion of residency. I was among the less than five percent to work and join a year later.

"How about for two reasons?" I ventured to say.

He took my response with a smile and said, "Two reasons it is."

"Training fatigue, and I needed to pay off a debt."

"How is that training fatigue today?" he asked with a chuckle.

"Strangely I missed the challenge, the books, the getting up early, the constant deadlines and so forth."

"And the debt, did you pay it off just to acquire another?"

"Paid in full on my way to acquire more sir." He had laughed heartily, seemingly impressed.

The interview was essentially over. The remaining time, Dr. Sanders spent talking of his exploits as a former deep-sea diver and rescuer. He spoke with great enthusiasm of his adventures in the jungle of Brazil as an infectious disease specialist, attending exotic infections while trying to eradicate others. He completed his boasting by welcoming me to his program as his fellow for 2011.

"I will make a master infectious diseases specialist out of you yet," was his last phrase to finalize the interview as he extended his hand in welcome.

That was two years ago; now he was telling a different story. When he was done speaking, he turned, attempting to leave the office. Except, there I was, standing in the doorway. Our eyes met. Mine spoke thousands of questions. He was serious and determined. He nodded a curt greeting while attempting to walk past me. If he was disappointed that I overheard his conversation, except for the mild red hue to both cheeks, he hid it well.

"Why should I not take my licensing boards?" My steady voice did not reflect what I felt: bewilderment and annoyance.

"You will not pass," he responded with assured finality. "And your failure will reflect badly on the school's standing."

I invited myself inside his office, afraid of lurching ears getting wind of my dilemma.

"Should I doubt the training that I received here at your University and at Mayo Clinic?" I responded.

He was quick in his assurance to the contrary, while lauding the excellency of the program, the eminence of the professors within its walls, and the well-earned respect of the institution.

"You're counting me out, even before I take the test. Why?"

"Your performance on the in-training practice test this year was dismal."

"That was only a practice test."

"But it closely mirrors the real boards," he replied.

"The boards are three months away."

"You propose to know three years' work in three months?"

"I have been studying all along."

"I doubt it will suffice. Take the year and study, and then you will be ready," he retorted with a hint of weariness in his voice.

The implication of waiting an entire year to take my exam was beginning to sink in: not being board certified was a disqualifying factor to work at many hospitals. On every application I filed, I would have to inform them that, while board eligible, I was uncertified. This was not a compliment, and not seen as the greatest way to start my professional work. What could I say to reassure him? He would not understand that faith in God, coupled with hard work, was unbeatable. This was my experience on which I based my entire existence, but he would not buy it.

While he was busy training me about infectious diseases, I was always looking for an opportunity to talk to him about creation and the plan of salvation. He did not hide his disinterest. He said he was a skeptic, and his rebuff was persistent. He refused every invitation to hear me sing.

"As long as it's in church and about the Bible and its Jesus, I will decline." He said that the closest he'd come to a church was looking at the cathedrals he visited all over Europe.

"The handbook stated," I said, "that all fellows are board-eligible upon completion of all requirements. I met all the requirements with above average grades, some superior."

"That is the case, but as your director, I recommend that you take an extra year and study before you take your fellowship boards examination." Here he was making sure I knew his word carried more weight than the handbook he helped to write, maybe rightly so.

THE LETTER

He looked unmoved as we stood looking at each other, the young facing the not-so-young, the well-seasoned doctor opposite the newly-taught. He knew that he needed to pass on the baton. I needed to reassure him that I was ready. His snow-white hair, the dark circles under his eyes, his permanent laugh line all helped tell the story of his 30 years of service to the health of humanity. Whatever I told Dr. Sanders in my defense would need to be self-deprecating and in deference to all he represented.

There was also a bigger factor pulling on my heart strings. I liked Dr. Sanders as a person. I saw him not only as the best infectious diseases doctor in my institution but also as one who had touched the lives of many, including mine. We all knew that he was a decent human being who deeply cared about his patients and the medical profession. Yet every man has a duty to fight for his survival. The challenge is how to do so while taking consideration of the other. I decided to make one last attempt to sway his decision.

"I will not let you down. After all, you trained me. I know how important the reputation of this institution is to you."

"Diane, it's a subspecialty board exam. They are killers." He sounded tired. "Other doctors will be coming to you for guidance. The final analysis from an infectious disease point of view will rest with you. There will be no room for error."

While he spoke, there was no meanness in his voice. His eyes told me he just wanted to make sure that I would pass the test at first attempt, and well. Whenever that feat is accomplished it puts the university at a whole new level at the time the institution's training program is re-evaluated. I was aware the graduating fellow two years prior had failed the prestigious exam. That may have factored into his decision of caution.

"I'll wait another year," I told him and exited his office.

Two weeks later, on the day of my graduation. I took the half-minute walk. I was handed a certificate stating I was now a diplomate in the area of infectious diseases. Dr. Sanders shook my hand and offered his congratulations.

"Kiddo, I've signed all the required papers for the exams. You're free to take your boards."

"I will not have to wait a year?"

"You will not have to wait a year," was all he said.

I never knew what brought about the change of heart, except to say that I was praying that God would do what was best for my life, and if waiting an entire year was best, then I would wait without grudge or complaints.

I knew I would pass. I had been studying since day one, and never stopped praying since that day on the Hill.

Three months later, impatiently, clumsily, with bated breath, I paced back and forth with phone in hand.

"Dr. Sanders, I passed the boards, first attempt, with eighty points to spare. I am now a Board-Certified Infectious Disease Specialist."

"There are times when I am happy to be proven wrong," he responded. "Your family should be proud of you."

The following day in Dr. Sanders' office I asked him, "Are you happy you chose to train me to receive the baton from your hand?"

He laughed the same proud laugh I heard countless times when his medical decision and judgment saved a life.

"You did a good job."

"I believe I did."

"This is it, kiddo." He extended his hand, but I hugged him instead.

"I'm finished. It's over."

"Dr. Vanhorne, it's never over! There is always something, but I believe you will find a way to succeed."

"Florida never looked so beautiful," I thought aloud.

Deus non potest percussum, I muttered as I exited his office. The lady mopping the floor eyed me suspiciously. I smiled self-consciously. I was quite sure she was not accustomed to seeing a doctor talking to herself and smiling.

Chapter 18

The Missionary

Santa Rita was a small, hidden rural village located in the mountains of Tamaulipas, Mexico, a place where perhaps a thousand inhabitants called home. It was one road in, the same road out. It was a village also in need of a physician. Doctors willing to volunteer or otherwise be assigned as part of their social services for a year was the only way this community received the medical attention they required. I accepted the assignment, along with the stipulation that I would start "as soon as possible." I did not know, though, that it meant reporting to work only a week after completing my training.

A month's notice would still have been too short a time to organize and dispose of items—way too burdensome to take with me to my new medical "adventure," as I was told it would be.

I was not told much about the village itself, nor the clinic in which I was to work, except that I would be provided a nurse, two free weekends per month, and a two-week holiday for the year. A stipend of three hundred pesos, the equivalent of $70 US, was the doctor's monthly allowance. I was not told, however, that running water and electricity were, at best, intermittent. I was also not made aware of the "uniqueness" of the village transportation: only one public bus. The bus would arrive in the village at 5:00 AM to begin its journey. It went through other small towns, collecting passengers as it bumped and lurched through rough terrain to its final destination, the city of San Fernando. It made its final return of the day at 6:00 PM. This limited schedule meant should I or any of the villagers miss the bus, finding overnight lodging in one of the city's tiny hotels, or with luck catch a ride from the few locals who own a private vehicle were our only options. Since money was a scarce commodity for overnight lodging, if for some reason we missed the bus or there was not enough room for all passengers, I often found myself fanning out at the roadside, hoping with luck to catch a glimpse of one of the villager's vehicles. They were not hard to miss as most were quite old, and looked as if any minute they would fall apart into a pile of smoke and rubble.

The day of my arrival at Santa Rita, as I entered the village square, kids were playing soccer barefoot. A few women were milling around, discreetly watching the passengers on the bus. Maybe news of my arrival brought them out? Maybe they were hoping to get a glimpse of me, the stranger soon to be a member of their community?

From the layout of the community, I could not miss which businesses were the key players. The grocery store was at the entrance of the town. It was a converted front patio of the owner's house, boxed in and painted bright yellow. I dare say, it made quite a splash. That was the shopping center for the little village. Once a week a truck would bring some fresh fruits and vegetables for us to buy.

I happened upon the local council meeting place. The sign was clearly placed for all to see. I suspected it was there that all decisions for the community were made by its leaders. Not too far was a bone-white church, the cross raised high on the steeple, making sure her identity was not mistaken. Right beside her was the school painted dark yellow. It bore a Mexican flag displaying its symbol of an eagle, perched over the cactus, eating a serpent. The houses were neatly lined up, almost in a circular pattern, each with its attached outside lavatory. I was fascinated and happy.

THE MISSIONARY

At last, there it was, my first official missionary posting! The clinic came into view. Small yet regal, maybe because it was to be not only my place of work but also my home for the next twelve months. Inside, I found two small medical examination rooms, but to me they were fabulous. A short passage area separated two adjoining bedrooms. One was for me, the other for the nurse. A tiny kitchen and an even smaller bathroom completed the magnificent place.

I was in my wonderful place of joy until I examined the scant supply of gloves, normal saline solutions, Tylenol, and the few boxes of antibiotics available. I breathed a sigh of relief after counting. It seemed we had enough to last a full week. My joy was short lived, however, when I was informed by the clinic steward that the clinic is restocked once a month by the health department. We were a little less than three weeks away before month's end.

"You will have to make do, just like those before you," said Christina, the clinic's caretaker.

It was hard to wrap my head around the notice that the gloves used for examination were to be recycled. Once used, they were to be washed, placed in the autoclave for sterilization, and then repackaged for reuse. But not even recycled gloves were enough to dampen the excitement for what the year would be like. Finally, they all came to examine the newest arrival to their community.

"Where are you from?" one asked.

"She has a weird accent," I overheard one saying.

I had grown accustomed to comments on the way I spoke Spanish as a native English speaker. A few smiles and giggles were not uncommon. I was content; at least I was understood.

"Is that your real hair," asked another, touching my long braids, without asking. I hoped my expression did not show my displeasure. Having my hair randomly touched was one of my pet peeves.

"She is pretty," said a little girl diving behind her mother's skirt. She followed up by asking if I was hungry. And even though I responded no, she did what I later learned to be very much part of the Mexican culture and handed me a bag with taco, admonishing me to eat before they were cold.

I must have passed inspection, since after that day I never lacked company. I was invited to all the events, including the monthly committee meeting where decisions were made for the village. I often had too many offers of help for whatever I needed to get done.

"You don't mind me calling you Dr. V? It's easier for me," said Carmen, the RN assigned to work with me for the year.

She was already busy arranging her room, installing pictures of family on the wall and was quick to point out her newly achieved RN certificate. I quickly nodded "yes" to the name change.

"Will you stay?" Carmen asked. It was clear she had heard. I was hoping she didn't. News traveled fast in the small neighboring towns.

"Yes, I'll stay," I responded, hoping I sounded convincing.

Faith and hope are wonderful things in the light of day; I was filled with both, at least until nightfall. I hated the dark. Most homes in the villages used lanterns which are put out while asleep. Streets lights were little to none. Pitch blackness usually hung over the village.

"Why did you leave the other clinic?" She eyed me curiously.

I had accepted a similar posting at a nearby village; however, on the day of my arrival the electricity was out, and though this was somewhat routine for villagers, for me it was not, so I took off before nightfall.

"Don't worry, I will be staying this time," I said, smiling reassuringly. I was not about to tell her I was quite spooked by the thought of sleeping in the dark in a new place.

Despite our limitations, things were off to a good start. Carmen and I breezed through our first five months working together, without any complications. No drama. Most of our cases were common, recurrent issues: poorly controlled diabetes, hypertension, flu, colds, etc. We were fast becoming pros on how to navigate the days without power and the weeks without running water. We were happy when the water and light stayed on two consecutive days in a row. It gave us time to gather and store water in a large container, restock our candles and refill our kerosene lanterns. These precious items were strategically placed in anticipation of the power outage, or lack of running water.

Along with offering medical care to the community, I was keen to embrace opportunities to share the creation-redemption story. Having no place to go, coupled with lack of consistent and reliable public transportation, I spent my free weekends gathering the local kids for story time. They loved, for instance, the action-packed hero stories about Daniel in the lion's den.

Carmen and I were beginning to breathe easy, and then we met Petra. The week before, we lost a patient; he didn't even make it to the clinic. He had a sudden headache and within minutes of the onset was dead. His autopsy showed a brain aneurysm. The tiny village where everybody knows everybody was still in deep mourning. They honor the victims' families by adhering to no music, no celebrations and they wear a long sad face if they happen upon the wife. When Petra, who was barely 18-years-old, pregnant with her first child, weak, pale, lethargic, looking woefully underweight, was carried into my under-prepared clinic for such a current medical state, saying I was anxious would be an understatement. My obstetric knowledge was that of a doctor who did two months rotation while in my transitional year in family medicine.

"I'm vomiting all the time," Petra said, her voice a tad above a whisper. She was approximately twelve to sixteen weeks pregnant and had spent the better half of those weeks vomiting and unable to eat, per her mother's report. She and her family tried home remedies before coming to the clinic. Trying home remedies first, before a doctor, was an unwritten rule for the village. Such practice cast its shadow of distress by the time they came to the clinic.

THE LETTER

A gangrenous foot was self-attended for weeks; a runner banging on the door at odd hours rushed me to the home of a patient in a diabetic coma after self-treating for days or to the hillside where the community drunk was found almost unconscious.

I had never prayed so fervently for help before my posting at the Santa Rita's Medical Clinic. There were times when I was truthfully in over my head, and times when I just wanted to sit down and cry — scream even.

My quick assessment of Petra led me to conclude severe hyperemesis gravidarum, malnutrition, dangerously low blood pressure, matched by the compensatory high heart rate, pale skin, and complaints of feeling profoundly weak and tired. Without labs, I could only guess, but I was sure that she was anemic, possibly in renal failure all due to significant dehydration and, likely, abnormal electrolytes, the cause of the vomiting. Both she and her unborn were at risk.

"She needed replacement hydration and nutrition a month ago." Carmen voiced my concerns while she feverishly tried to get IV access for fluids.

"We need to get her to the city hospital for obstetric care."

"But her husband is away at work. What will we do for transportation?"

"Like before, we will cast ourselves on the mercy of the village leader."

In vain, I tried explaining to Petra and her mother that the clinic lacked what she needed, and that the city hospital was the best option. Her response was a firm, "No!" My mind was working overtime. "How can I convince both?" I wondered aloud.

One more day of vomiting, one more day without eating could mean the undoing of both mother and child. "The unborn infant may have already suffered irreversible damage already," I thought to myself.

THE MISSIONARY

"Why won't she go?" I asked Carmen, puzzled. There were many cultural dynamics I was yet to learn.

"Most of your patients have never left the village, much less stayed away overnight," she responded.

"Will it help if you accompany her?"

"What if we lose electricity in the night? I hate reminding you of your fear of the dark."

"I've long ago faced my fears," I responded.

Carmen finally got on board. I lowered the stethoscope over the patient's belly and gently placed the listening device in the soon-to-be mother's ear. First, fear followed by curiosity. Her eyes lit up, followed by a wide smile. She heard the baby's heart beat for the first time. It worked; she was ready to go where she and her baby could receive better care. I breathed a sigh of relief. It took me a while to steady my trembling hands.

Five months later, Petra handed me a tiny but beautiful girl. She looked small for her age.

"Here!" She literally thrust the baby into my arms. As I looked closer, I realized that half of one of the baby's arms was missing. She was phocomelia; I was hesitant to look up at Petra's face, afraid of what I may find there. She reached up and took her child and then I saw her eyes: like any mother, they spoke of love and joy.

"Her name is Bella," she said. "Bella" means "beautiful" in English. She thanked me and retreated with her baby, secure in her arms.

"What future will this village offer Bella with one and half limb?" I asked Carmen.

"I'll leave you, Madame Doctor, to worry about the implications," she replied, "but I am off to my exercise. You coming?"

I exhaled deeply, marking one more day off the calendar. As I removed my white coat and attempted to hang it in its place, the abbreviated words TGBTG (To God Be the Glory) caught my eyes. I had them engraved on the inside of my coat. The imprint was fading. The same abbreviation, TGBTG, was scattered on most, if not all, of my medical books.

To God Be the Glory, an emblem of how I wanted my life to be. Such a noble thought but the reality was sadly lacking. Weary from an extraordinarily long day's work, I acknowledged that I was very lonely and often running on empty. Except for the knowledge of medicine and the patients I cared for, I often felt adrift.

"Dr. Vanhorne, a call from Dr. Lucas." The clinic ward's voice brought me back to the present.

"Take a message," I mouthed to her as I watched through the window as Carmen started her exercise routine, slow and unhurried.

I had promised I would join her.

"He insists," she whispered, her hand covering the mouth piece. "Says he has follow-up questions on books you gave him."

My ears perked up. Dr. Lucas and I somewhat Lucas and I somewhat lost touch after graduation, but not before I had given him some books, including one called *The Great Controversy*, by Ellen White (Mountain View, California: Pacific Press Publishing Association, 1950).

"I am beginning to understand," was his first comment after we said our hello.

"Great!"

"I decided to swap my Darwin books for the creation-redemption story."

"I'm happy to hear."

"My heart never really took to the evolution theories, and my mind rejected its reasoning," he declared.

Chapter 19

What Is One Thing You'd Do Knowing You'd Never Fail?

And that's how it began, a proposal followed by a wedding. Lucas, now my husband, decided that he must attend his baby sister's 15-year-old birthday party.

"It's too much a part of my family culture to miss," he responded to my plea not to go.

I had such unease about the trip, but half-heartedly supported his travel plans after failing to convince him to stay home. My apprehension became worse as the night before his departure, I dreamed that the plane he was on fell from the sky and I was walking among its debris in search of him.

"Pray and rest," he encouraged me, his voice as always calm, unhurried, never stressed. His kind green eyes held a hint of smile, a smile that always reassured me.

"I think you ate too many tacos last night," he teased. "I will be back in three days, just in time for you to go back to work," he said gleefully as he grabbed his suitcase and headed toward the waiting cab.

However, Lucas' promised three days snowballed. Six weeks later he was yet to return home. After attending his sister's birthday celebration in Mexico, he was denied re-entry to the USA. The reason? He was in the process of his green card application and, per the lawyer, any person going through that process is not allowed to travel outside of the US without first getting prior approval to travel. Lucas did not get prior approval.

Things were close to becoming unbearable: a new job in Jacksonville, Florida, three kids, and mountains of boxes still waiting to be unpacked. So, I did what I could.

The idea was that my current situation did not take God by surprise. That's what my friend Mrs. Banton, a retired teacher, told me. Mrs. Banton, a widow, spent her time praying and visiting the shut-ins and new mothers like me.

"That still does not obliterate the frustration I am feeling," I said.

The immigration lawyer's feedback was less than encouraging, stating there wasn't really anything he could do. His final conclusion was that Lucas would have to wait out the time for his green card approval. That was almost a year out.

After pondering the rather bleak report, the usual midweek prayer meeting never seemed more urgent or needed. I made my way to church with two children in close pursuit and the other sucking his thumb in the stroller. My friend and colleague Alex, a cardiologist, who happened to be on her week vacation, came along for moral support. Her son was my eldest son's age and made a good distraction for him. Of his siblings, he seemed to be missing his father most. It helped that Alex's husband was an ER doctor and worked the night shift. Every day for a week she was purposeful in her effort to keep my mind at ease, especially in the evening hours. Things tended to seem more intolerable as the day ended.

During a prayer meeting, one of the worshippers sitting opposite my chair handed me a small piece of paper. On it he had written the question: "What would you do today if you knew you could not fail?"

The word, "fail," caught my attention the most. Failing was what I felt that I was doing all these six weeks alone with three kids, and a new and beautiful yet wickedly busy hospital routine to juggle.

As never before I could identify with that word. It was only the day before that I had dropped off the two oldest kids to school and drove the twenty minutes to work when I realized what I had done.

I was about to exit the highway to the hospital when I heard a rustling sound in the back and turned to greet two happy deep brown eyes peering back at me, those of my infant son, sucking his thumb with great contentment. In my rush, I had forgotten to drop him off at daycare. I blamed my lapse in memory to still reeling from the "adventure" of the weekend. I was on call: Lucas' forced absence meant that I needed outside help. Except, it was the weekend and my go-to child care provider had pre-arranged travel plans. The friend and colleague whom I trust to babysit was also on hospital duty for the weekend. Family was thousands of miles away.

To solve my problem, the doctors' lounge was converted into a playpen and my colleagues coming off night duties did "guard duty" while I cared for the sick. But it was not without its moments of stress. I smiled back at my son, Matt. I wished I could experience the peace and calm demeanor he displayed, in spite of all that was happening. It was an easy 20-minute drive back to the daycare, except it was Monday, peak traffic time. Hours later, I returned to work close to tears.

"God please, help!" I prayed in desperation. "We cannot cope without Lucas. Show me what to do."

I re-read the note from the stranger: "What would you do today If you knew you could not fail?" The question swirled in my thoughts. In my current state, I could think of nothing that I would not fail at. During Lucas's six-week hold up in Mexico, I placed enough fruitless calls, followed enough dead leads, to people in high places and influence whom I was sure could and would help and was beginning to realize there was absolutely nothing humanly possible that I or anyone I knew could do to change his current situation. But, before I could despair, memories of a recent event where God showed Himself strong on behalf of my family came to mind.

THE LETTER

It was Christmas Eve, and I was on call overnight in the hospital. I was scheduled to work for the entire Christmas and New Year's season. I had Thanksgiving break off, so now was payback time. In the spirit of the season, one of my colleagues had offered to cover my shift for two hours so that I could at least have dinner with my family. Arrangements were in place for my patients to be cared for while I enjoyed the two cherished hours. I quickly exited the hospital toward the car where Lucas and the kids were waiting. The conversations were happy as we made our way toward the restaurant, where he had made the reservation. I could smell and taste my favorite dish in my mouth as we turned into the restaurant driveway and attempted to park, except that the car's transmission was jammed. The parking lot was situated on a hill; thus, the car was perched awkwardly, as if getting ready to roll backwards and out of control.

Lucas and I were caught up in the stress of the moment, trying to figure out how to get the gear shift to work, in order to get me back to work on time, get himself and the kids home, and get the car to the garage to be fixed. It did not help that it was Christmas Eve and cab service was slow and sparse. Back then there was no Uber, no Lyft, nor smartphone apps to tell me the best move.

"Mom, Dad, let's pray and ask God to help," our eldest son requested.

"Soon, honey," we responded and kept feverishly working to come up with a plan, realizing time was closing in for me to return to the hospital. All thoughts of a fun meal were now out the window. The smell of food suddenly became unwelcome, and for the first time, I realized that the restaurant was not only small with minimal upkeep, but that this part of town was quite run down and potentially dangerous at night.

Minutes later, again: "Mommy, God can help us. Let's pray, Mommy."

WHAT IS ONE THING YOU'D DO KNOWING YOU'D NEVER FAIL?

"Maxwell, be patient," the voice was stern. Minutes later I noticed an unusual hushed silence emanating from the back of the car where all the kids were sitting. I looked in their direction, expecting some mischief. Rather, to our pleasant surprise, we found Maxwell kneeling, head down, eyes closed, with his other siblings in prayer. The prayer was simple.

"Dear Jesus, please help Mom and Dad with the car problem."

They had barely said "Amen" when we saw a taxi that we did not call circling our car.

"You need help?" the driver asked.

"Do we need help?" Lucas responded. "We sure do."

As he drove us to our destination, he explained he had run his last shift and was planning to have an early evening with his family when he felt impressed to circle around for one more shift and was unwillingly guided in our direction. He not only took my family home and dropped me off back at the hospital, but he waited for AAA to escort the disabled vehicle to the mechanic shop—all for one cost. All this was an answer to a child who prayed when his parents were too busy arguing and stressing.

So, to answer the question, what would I do if I knew that I could not fail? I came up blank after giving it much thought, but I chose prayer. I fasted, prayed, prayed and fasted some more. And every day at 6pm, Mrs. Banton would call to pray with me and remind me that God would bring my husband home soon.

Days later I felt impressed to call and check up on a friend. Our line of communication was broken.

"Call the Congresswoman for your area," was her response to my dilemma. "God can use whomever He wants. He has people in high places."

I was hesitant. Who am I that a US Congresswoman should intervene and call the US embassy on my family's behalf? In my humanity, I had forgotten what God did for me in the past.

I made the call. Within an hour, I filled out and faxed back the information requested by the congresswoman's office. Next, it was a letter of support from the university hospital stating my work depends on my family being together. The next day the embassy office called Lucas in to be re-interviewed. The same day he was on a flight back to Florida. It would have been too easy an ending except two hours later I was still at the airport waiting. Lucas missed his connecting flight. After everything, he had managed to end up at the wrong boarding gate! He was placed on standby for the next flight out. But we were beyond joy because he was on his way home.

Months after Lucas' glad return, the simple question lingers: What would you do today if you knew you could not fail? Direct a major motion picture, open a business, get a degree? But those earthly dreams are too small, too finite. Go for the big leagues. Attempt something that failure is assured, unless God intervenes.

I think of my journey of becoming a medical doctor – the one that started with an audacious letter written to God when I was too young to talk myself out of it. I have seen so many glimpses of His victory when I should have failed. Because of this journey, I now believe we can fail at nothing when God is in it. Failure to me is a myth; it's rather who we believe, and how we adapt to what we encounter in our journey. For me, it is about He who made us, His power in us to survive, to persevere. It's also about faith and hope.

Chapter 20

Still Standing

"Oh, God, our help in ages past, our hope for years to come" (Watts, 1719). I stood at the door, looking at Ma-ma. As was her custom, her Bible was opened in her lap. "Our shelter from the stormy blast, and our eternal home," she hummed.

She looked different. She looked the same. Not quite as strong, but she remained strong. Her years of toil and labor left their marks. The proof was there, in her bent frame. Her hair was now fully snow white and it looked thin. Her voice, however, was strong and with the flow of the now memorized hymn, told me that her mind remained untouched. Her eyes were undimmed as she read her Bible aloud without aid.

Then she saw me: her expression will remain indescribable.

"Diane is that you? I knew God would bring you back to me. I told your mom I had a feeling it would be today."

Almost twenty years had passed. I fell at her feet and wept; all the years of bottled up emotions rushed forth like a dam, breaking the levy of strength that I had carefully crafted. Around her, I was the child who had left.

"It was so hard, Ma-ma!" I gasped between sobs.

Placing her hand on my head she blessed me. "Promise to never leave the path that leads to God." Her voice, though soft, was urgent.

"Where else would I go?"

THE LETTER

"Promise either way."

I pulled myself together enough to promise. She spoke faith into me, stating that God is still at work in my life, enlarging my path, guiding my feet and prospering my efforts. As before, she was quick to remind me that God prospering me did not mean acquisition of earthly goods like fame and money, but rather joy, peace, and a sound mind.

Praying, she asked God to pour a double portion of His blessing into my life. While she prayed, I wept, and she cradled my head in her lap just like she did the day I left her.

"One day," she promised, "you will see more clearly God's leading, and you will come to trust His presence more fully."

She made me promise to raise my kids after God's order.

I presented my new family. She placed her hand on each of my sons' heads and lingered a bit longer on my daughter's and blessed them.

"You have a husband who loves you. I like him." Her smile said it all.

Together we reminisced about the Hill, the journey, and those who had died, gone on ahead to rest, waiting for the resurrection.

"Only God knows the end of all things," she said.

"Only God knows the end of all things," I repeated.

"God. His imprint in the smallest detail of our human lives."

"The master mover, like a world class chess player whose move can never be matched or outdone. Checkmate!"

Epilogue

It was Monday morning, and although it was the beginning of the work week, it already felt used, tired, old, and a bit gloomy.

"It's raining on the inside," I muttered to my colleague Dr. Pavel who like me was busy reviewing and contemplating his newly printed list of patients for the day.

"Raining on the inside" was a phrase I used to describe the hospital when it was overflowing with very complex, complicated, and moribund patients. Today it was raining. It didn't help that I was starting the work day tired. I suspected the same for Dr. Pavel. This was day eight of what would be a twelve-day straight work schedule. I was already in a low-level state of exhaustion.

"What was that?" Dr. Pavel asked distractedly. He was multitasking between getting updates about his 4-month-old daughter at home with a fever and reviewing his patient's chart.

Working together for the past four years, Dr. Pavel and I witnessed some of the most consequential and emotionally vexing medical scenarios. We were still processing the recent loss of one of our colleagues, a neurosurgeon, to suicide. As a side note, if the reported statistics are to be believed, every day a medical doctor dies by suicide. However, the silence surrounding the untold story of suicide among us healthcare professionals remains remarkably so… mostly silent. Unknown. Unreported. Maybe it's too much of a paradox to understand when the healers themselves are in need of healing.

"A rural town in a developing country was where I hoped to practice medicine," was my complaint.

THE LETTER

"What is so wrong with the comforts of Florida?" he asked, failing to hide his thinly veiled tone of surprise.

He was right, Florida is a beauty. Her sun-kissed beaches are beyond comparison. Her theme parks are unmatched. Her people are kind. So "the wrong" was not with Florida.

Dr. Pavel was an uncommon person. He was extremely aware that he was considered one of the fortunate few who escaped his place of birth and enjoyed true success. He fully embraced his adopted home, the US, a place where for many immigrants is "earth's promised land." Except for his difficulty in the pronunciation of the letter "x" from that of "s" (example "massimum" for "maximum") he successfully assimilated into his new culture as a respected medical doctor. His homeland, Cuba, with all its reported limitations and humbug, became a distant memory, if only on the surface, as he often conjured up stories of home. His talks of the old vintage cars, the music, and the food made it clear that the web of memories would remain in his heart forever.

If there was an award for camaraderie, Dr. Pavel would have gotten all the votes. The song "He's a Jolly Good Fellow" was written with him in mind. Compassion, kindness, and gratitude were modeled in his day-to-day practice of medicine. These qualities may account for the love his patients showed him. He was a hard act to follow.

With all that said, I however doubted even he, the famed "jolly good fellow," the poster child for great assimilation, would understand how deeply unsettled I was feeling of late. After all, there was nothing in the "sunny, happy, I-got-this" disposition I displayed at work that would have given the tiniest hint to the unhappiness that was brewing on the inside. And like Pavel said, "the comforts of Florida." What was there to be unhappy about was a reasonable question. Yet there were the ants, which were bringing back memories of childhood heroes.

EPILOGUE

Mother Teresa was one of my main heroes growing up. The dress. The scarf. The head wear. The way she would hold patients' hands, kneeling beside them. Working like her was my ultimate ideal. I was going to "change the world" as a missionary doctor. My impact would be unquestioned. To heal, to make humanity right was my all-encompassing idealistic goal. Instead, here I was just juggling and hustling like everyone else. There was no escaping the luxury and prestige that comes with being a dual specialized medical doctor in the USA. There was to be no going off as a missionary to New Guinea or Somalia without a huge family meeting, compromise, and agreement.

"One dollar," was what I had jotted down for my monthly wages on my first job application.

"Labor laws will not allow it," the human resources representative informed me. "Either way, how would you live?" she asked, indicating I needed to put a realistic salary.

"It would be up to God," was my answer.

Forward to today, how could I tell my colleague that I was losing my enthusiasm, that I was marginally unhappy, that there were days when I was convinced the life of a medical doctor was not for me, that I could no longer quiet the feeling that I was not where the need was greatest, that I was not needed? How could I tell him that the passion to create positive and lasting change, the desire to make an impact, the will to connect fully with all my patients, had all but left me behind? Could I tell Pavel, my colleague, how a patient's tears no longer represented the tears of all humanity for me? To watch a soul pass into eternity was losing its reverence and sacredness, and was now just fading into numbers. My inner voice was advising me to quit.

"I was doing the work only to clear the bills," my conscience sometimes whispered. That accusatory voice was louder at the end of the tough days. It was loudest when I was tired and nearly burned out, merciless. Those were inner conversations that were best left unspoken, even to the best of colleagues.

It did not help that recent tragic events further solidified my feeling of haunted forlorn. Alice was not just another patient. I knew her well. I walked with her through her open heart surgery. Her infected tricuspid heart valve was replaced with pork skin to keep it working. For two years, she refrained from abusing illicit drugs, and dutifully kept all her appointments with me.

"See, Doctor, I promised you I would come, and here I am," was her usual phrase. "I sometimes miss going to another doctor's appointment, but I will never miss ours," she would announce proudly.

I knew better than to get emotionally attached to my patients, but Alice was different. She tried so very hard to kick her drug addiction. Her resolve won me over. Soon I would be checking in to make sure she took her medication. She was showing up for rehabilitation sessions but keeping her court days and parole appointments became my concern.

The day Alice died had been my day off from the hospital. She came in for fever and mild shortness of breath. When she found out I was off duty and that she would be seen by another doctor, she signed out against medical advice. By the time she tried to make it back to the hospital, she had collapsed. Her infected heart valve had simply burst open. Alice was only 24 years old. For a very long time, I wished I were on call that day. I might have convinced her not to sign herself outt of the hospital. It may not have made a difference, but still I wish.

"What's so wrong with working with state-of-the-art technology at one of the best metropolitan hospitals?" Dr. Pavel brought me back to the issues at hand.

"Where would we be without technology?" I offered. "Nothing against its wonders," I continued.

"Let's debrief," he responded, leading me away from listening ears.

"The majority of the patients I see are young with an existence wrapped up in the trauma of drug addiction. And I by extension get to share that trauma. In them I see what we all could have become except that our life experiences were different. They promise me, wholeheartedly, to quit. I naively believe them until they come back a week later, worse off or dead. The reality is soul crushing," I explained. "Nothing I do seems to make a difference. Resources are extremely limited. Getting them the help they need to quit is like fighting World War II alone," I lamented. "This is not the practice of medicine I envisioned. Even the prayers I pray on their behalf seem to go unanswered. It's discouraging. Sometimes I am overwhelmed with the feeling of helplessness."

"Maybe this is your mission field ... your Mother Teresa moment. In addition to your expertise, they need compassion, empathy, and love. Those are the things I see in you and you hold nothing back, not even your vulnerability. You are well suited for this demographic," he said with certainty.

But I didn't want this demographic. Surely my mission field could not be one fraught with such depth of personal sadness, tightly laced with a sense of impotence. The opportunity for meaningful change was nowhere in sight. My desperately wishing away the day the patient first encountered the cursed, double-cursed substance that worked to their demise was like a fool's comfort.

I was not the ideal person for this moment; I was sure of that. It was hard, emotionally that is. I usually get too close and too involved. I failed the aloof detachment test, starting long ago back in my training days in Texas. The result was that every time one of my patients died, the questions were always the same:

Was there more that could have been done? Did I do my best? Were they loved? Did I love them? Did I see their suffering? Did I embrace our common humanity? Did I judge them because of their addiction? Becoming immune to their plight was a choice I could never reconcile.

"A human tragedy," Dr. Pavel stated as if reading my thoughts. "They are unemployed so cannot financially take care of themselves," he fussed, "uninsured and cannot secure the rehabilitation services they are in desperate need of to recover, and all too commonly, many have undiagnosed and untreated mental health disorders, sometimes since childhood," he lamented.

"A good number are often homeless, challenging the policy of a safe hospital discharge. It's inhumane to release them back to the streets," was my reply.

"While society overlooks them," he added. "With time even their families walk away."

"The moms I find are most times the only exception--they stay," I reminded Pavel.

"This may be your mission field," he nudged. "Your wish of a rural town in a developing country may be lacking, but the need, and the suffering, is very much one and the same."

The task at hand is great. Are we up to it? That was the unspoken question left hanging.

By now, we were conversing in his full native language: Spanish, his comfort zone. Strangely enough, although a native English speaker, Spanish was also my comfort zone. My strongest emotions, it seems, were better expressed by way of speaking in Spanish.

"Keep laying it all down. The striving to make it better and your smarts, that's enough for the task." His "Spanglish" was now coming through loud and clear as the conversation waned.

"You think so?"

"This is your mission field. You're well suited for the task."

"You think so?"

"I know so. I know no one who is as naturally better equipped as you are."

"Is weeping in the car at the day's end also part of it?"

"If only our cars could speak. The poor steering wheel has enough beating for a lifetime."

"It's emotional involvement ... there is no getting away."

"It's enormous."

EPILOGUE

"It is enormous and you are well suited; just remember not to take it home"

And while I felt Dr. Pavel was asking the impossible, part of me knew he was right. I was well suited. After all, I was my grandmother's child. Like her, nothing was done without love, a touch of God, and an unbreakable determination

Faces of my beloved patients began to flash in my mind; memories of our interactions invaded my thoughts. At that moment, I realized that It was not only my friend and colleague who was earnestly trying to encourage me but my inner man as well. God Himself was reminding me of that letter--our letter.

Maybe, in small increments, I was making a difference, maybe I was already complying my Schindler's list. One patient at a time. No fanfare. In obscure unsung moments, I must, again and again, remind my patients--the beautiful, young, desperate drug addict; the depressed, anxious teen who feels hopeless--that their lives are as valuable and as meaningful as the man who landed on the moon and as the mind who invented the wheel. That their brains are also capable of generating new pathways to healing, that they too can dream and create with the help of science, the passage of time and, of course, with the help of the One who created them in the first place.

I have concluded that the practice of medicine by its very nature is emotional and heartbreaking, all-encompassing and demanding. I have also concluded that it is impossible to measure one's impact for good as a mender of the broken; yet there are glimpses, beautiful moments when I sense that I have inspired someone to hope, to take courage, to desire to live fully, to seek change, and to press forward.

"Are you ready? They are waiting." Dr. Pavel interrupted my thoughts.

"I am ready."

CPSIA information can be obtained
at www.ICGtesting.com
Printed in the USA
LVHW081554051220
673100LV00010B/77